The BLUE PLAQUE Guide

English ⌗ Heritage

journeyman press
London • Concord, Mass

First published by the GLC

This edition first published in 1991
by Journeyman Press
345 Archway Road, London, N6 5AA
and 141 Old Bedford Road, Concord, MA 01742, USA
in association with English Heritage, Chesham House,
30 Warwick Street, London, W1R 5RD

British Library Cataloguing in Publication Data
The Blue Plaque Guide.
 1. London. Blue plaques
 942.1

  ISBN 1-85172-005-7

Library of Congress Cataloging-in-Publication Data
applied for.

Designed by Ray Addicott

Typeset by Archetype, Stow-on-the-Wold
Printed and bound in the UK by Billing and Sons Ltd, Worcester

Contents

FOREWORD

Lord Montagu of Beaulieu

When English Heritage was asked to take over the commemorative plaques scheme in Greater London in 1986 it was the proud inheritor of a tradition going back for 120 years.

The blue plaques on buildings where famous people have lived have become as familiar a part of the London scene as the Changing of the Guard or red telephone boxes. They evoke interest from residents and visitors alike, and the number of enquiries we receive from far-flung parts of the world testifies to the popularity of the scheme.

Whenever I attend unveiling ceremonies I am always moved by the pleasure which the erection of a plaque clearly gives to so many people. Conversely, of course, I am aware that we have to disappoint some people by not accepting their suggestions, but I am certain that the balance is on the credit side.

Looking at a representative sample of the plaques which have been erected by English Heritage over the past four years, I hope you will agree that we have maintained the variety and interest of the scheme. T.S. Eliot's last home in Kensington, the birthplace of Viscount Montgomery of Alamein, the small flat overlooking the Thames where Jerome K. Jerome wrote *Three Men in a Boat*, the home of the great clown Grimaldi in Exmouth Market, the house where Jawaharlal Nehru stayed when a student at the Inner Temple, and the family hotel where the French novelist Emile Zola lived when in exile as a result of the Dreyfus Affair, all have a fascination which only an association with the famous can give them, and all are now distinguished by the familiar circular blue-and-white plaque.

This booklet contains a list of all the surviving plaques which were erected by the Royal Society of Arts, the London County Council, the Greater London Council and English Heritage, nearly 600 in all. For those of you who live in London I hope it will add to your enjoyment of the city as you go about your work and leisure pursuits, and for those of you who are visitors I hope it will enhance the pleasure of your stay.

Lord Montagu of Beaulieu
Chairman
English Heritage

INTRODUCTION

The last edition of the *Blue Plaque Guide* was published by the Greater London Council in 1976 and has long been out of print. This new edition follows the same basic format as its predecessor and consists of a list of plaques arranged alphabetically by the names of the persons commemorated, followed by indexes arranged by London borough, by street and by vocation. The information given under each entry in the main body of the Guide usually reproduces the wording on the plaque itself. In a few cases additional details are given which do not appear on the plaque. The full address, including the London postal district where appropriate, is given, and those houses which are open to the public are also indicated.

Users should note that this Guide lists all the plaques existing at 30 September 1990 which were erected by the Royal Society of Arts, the London County Council, the Greater London Council and English Heritage, together with a few which were originally erected privately but which have been subsequently 'adopted' as 'official' plaques. There are other plaques in London erected by local authorities, by societies and by private individuals which are not listed here, and the fact that a plaque to a famous person does not appear in this list does not mean that there is no plaque or other memorial to that person anywhere in London.

HISTORICAL NOTE

The Royal Society of Arts was the first body to act on a suggestion that commemorative plaques should be erected at the homes of famous people who had lived in London, and its first plaque was erected in 1867 at Byron's birthplace in Holles Street (since demolished). The Society had put up 36 plaques by 1901, when the London County Council took over the scheme. The LCC's first plaque was that to Lord Macaulay at Holly Lodge, Campden Hill, Kensington (also demolished). By 1965, when the scheme was transferred to the Greater London Council, there were 298 plaques in existence, over a third of them put up in the last 12 years of the LCC's existence. The GLC continued the scheme, extending it into the areas of outer London not covered by the LCC.

The Local Government Act of 1985 provided for the transfer of some of the functions of the GLC to English Heritage, including the erection of commemorative plaques in London, the first time that the blue plaque scheme had been included in an Act of Parliament. Since 1 April 1986 39 plaques have been erected by English Heritage. At 30 September 1990 there were 572 plaques in existence comprising 13 erected by the Royal Society of Arts, 249 by the LCC, 262 by the GLC, 39 by English Heritage and 9 erected by others and incorporated into the scheme. The earliest plaques now surviving are those to John Dryden in Gerrard Street and to Napoleon III in King Street, St James's, both erected by the Royal Society of Arts in 1875.

The purpose of the scheme has generally been to draw attention to buildings of interest because of their associations with famous people rather than to provide an honours list of worthy people. Although some of the earlier plaques mark the sites of demolished buildings, in more recent years it has been the invariable practice to erect a plaque only when the house in which a famous person lived is still standing. A number of plaques, however, mark the sites of famous buildings or historical events.

The Royal Society of Arts' first plaque was deep blue, with white lettering, but most of those erected before 1900 were a chocolate brown in colour and made by Minton. Between 1903 and 1921 the LCC experimented with a number of designs made in stone and metal as well as glazed terracotta, but in 1921 glazed Doulton ware was adopted as standard. The plainer design used in more recent years was chosen in 1937, with the white border added in 1939. In 1955 manufacture was taken over from Doulton by Carters, later Poole Pottery, and in 1982 by Alan Dawson Special Ceramics. Most plaques conform to the standard $19\frac{1}{2}$-inch-diameter circular blue and white design, now made in glazed earthenware, but a number of special designs in other materials have sometimes been made to meet particular circumstances.

When considering suggestions for plaques, the LCC at first took each case on an *ad hoc* basis. In 1954, however, criteria were established against which suggestions were evaluated; with minor amendments, those criteria have been adopted by English Heritage and are set out below.

All questions about the plaques and suggestions for new ones should be addressed to the London Division of English Heritage at Chesham House, 30 Warwick Street, London W1R 5RD. Proposers of plaques should, however, be aware that there is currently a long list of outstanding suggestions awaiting consideration, and that it is likely to be some time before any action can be taken on any new suggestions.

SELECTION CRITERIA

English Heritage has adopted the following principles for the guidance of those who wish to suggest the erection of commemorative plaques in London:

(a) English Heritage will erect plaques on buildings in Greater London associated with famous people in those cases where one of the following requirements is met:
(i) There shall be reasonable grounds for believing that the subjects are regarded as eminent by a majority of members of their own profession or calling.
(ii) They shall have made some important positive contribution to human welfare or happiness.
(iii) They shall have had such exceptional and outstanding personalities that the well-informed passer-by immediately recognises their names.
(iv) They deserve recognition.

(b) Without exception, proposals for the commemoration of famous people shall not be considered until they have been dead for 20 years or until the centenary of birth, whichever is the earlier.

(c) Plaques shall not be erected on the sites of former houses occupied by famous people, but consideration may be given to erecting plaques on reconstructed buildings which present an exact facsimile frontage on the identical site.

(d) Proposals will, however, be considered for the commemoration of sites of special historical interest.

(e) A building shall not be marked solely because it figures in a work of fiction.

(f) Although most plaques are erected on houses associated with famous people, the erection of plaques on blocks of flats is not excluded.

(g) A plaque shall generally take the form of a circular ceramic plaque about 20 inches in diameter with white lettering on a blue background. A different design may be used if for special reasons such a course is deemed appropriate.

The following additional principles have been adopted for guidance when plaques to foreigners are under consideration:

(h) They should be of international reputation or of significant standing in their own countries.

(i) Their time in London should have been a significant period, in time or in importance, within their life and work.

(j) The form of name, forename or title in the inscription on a plaque should be in accordance with that given in a standard English work of reference, or as would be readily recognisable to a reasonably well-informed passer-by.

Although all plaque suggestions falling within the criteria will be considered, English Heritage reserves the right to determine priorities among suggestions received.

The BLUE PLAQUE Guide

ADAM, J.
See ADELPHI TERRACE

ADAM, Robert (1728–1792),
architect; Thomas HOOD (1799–1845), poet; John
GALSWORTHY (1867–1933), novelist and playwright; Sir
James BARRIE (1860–1937), dramatist; and other eminent
artists and writers lived here.

1–3 Robert Street, Adelphi, WC2
Westminster   1950

ADAMS, Henry Brooks
See UNITED STATES EMBASSY

ADELPHI TERRACE
This building stands on the site of Adelphi Terrace built by
the brothers ADAM in 1768–1774. Famous residents in the
Terrace include Topham (1739–1780), friend of Dr Johnson
and Lady Diana BEAUCLERK (1734–1808), amateur artist;
David GARRICK (1717–1779), actor; Richard D'OYLY
CARTE (1844–1901), Savoy Opera promoter; Thomas
HARDY (1840–1928), poet and novelist and George Bernard
SHAW (1856–1950), author and playwright. The London
School of Economics and the Savage Club also had their
premises here.

*Supersedes separate plaques to David Garrick at No.5 Adelphi Terrace, and
the brothers Adam at No.4, destroyed during the demolition of the Terrace in
1936.*

The Adelphi, WC2
Westminster   1952

ALEXANDER, Sir George (1858–1918),
actor-manager, lived here.

57 Pont Street, SW1
Kensington and Chelsea   1951

ALEXANDRA PALACE
See TELEVISION

ALLENBY, Field Marshal Edmund Henry Hynman, Viscount (1861–1936),
lived here 1928–1936.

24 Wetherby Gardens, SW5
Kensington and Chelsea   1960

ALMA-TADEMA, Sir Laurence, OM (1836–1912),
painter, lived here 1886–1912.

44 Grove End Road, St. John's Wood, NW8
Westminster   1975

ANDERSON, Dr Elizabeth Garrett
See GARRETT ANDERSON

ARKWRIGHT, Sir Richard (1732–1792),
industrialist and inventor, lived here.

8 Adam Street, WC2
Westminster   1984

ARNE, Thomas (1710–1778),
composer, lived here.

31 King Street, Covent Garden, WC2
Westminster   1988

ARNOLD, Sir Edwin (1832–1904),
poet and journalist, lived and died here.

31 Bolton Gardens, SW5
Kensington and Chelsea   1931

ARNOLD, Matthew (1822–1888),
poet and critic, lived here.

2 Chester Square, SW1
Westminster   1954

ASHFIELD, Albert Henry Stanley, Lord Ashfield (1874–1948),
first Chairman of London Transport, lived here.

43 South Street, Mayfair, W1
Westminster   1984

ASQUITH, Herbert Henry, 1st Earl of Oxford and Asquith (1852–1928),
statesman, lived here.

20 Cavendish Square, W1
Westminster   1951

ASTAFIEVA, Princess Seraphine (1876–1934),
ballet dancer, lived and taught here.

152 King's Road, SW3
Kensington and Chelsea   1968

ASTOR, Nancy (1879–1964),
first woman to sit in Parliament, lived here.

4 St. James's Square, SW1
Westminster   1987

ATTLEE, Richard Clement (1883–1976),
Prime Minister, lived here.

17 Monkhams Avenue, Woodford Green
Redbridge   1984

AVEBURY, Baron: Sir John Lubbock (1834–1913),
scientist, born here.

29 Eaton Place, SW1
Westminster   1935

BADEN-POWELL, Robert (1857–1941),
Chief Scout of the World, lived here.

9 Hyde Park Gate, SW7
Kensington and Chelsea   1972

BAGEHOT, Walter (1826–1877),
writer, banker and economist, lived here.

12 Upper Belgrave Street, SW1
Westminster   1967

BAILLIE, Joanna,
poet and dramatist, born 1762, died 1851, lived in this house for nearly fifty years.

Bolton House, Windmill Hill, NW3
Camden   1900

BAIRD, John Logie (1888–1946),
first demonstrated television in this house in 1926.

22 Frith Street, W1
Westminster   1951

BAIRD, John Logie (1888–1946),
television pioneer, lived here.

3 Crescent Wood Road, Sydenham, SE26
Lewisham   1977

BAIRNSFATHER, Bruce (1888–1959),
cartoonist, lived here.

1 Sterling Street, off Montpelier Square, SW7

Westminster   1981

BALDWIN, Stanley (1867–1947),
Earl Baldwin of Bewdley, Prime Minister, lived here.

93 Eaton Square, SW1

Westminster   1969

BALFE, Michael William (1808–1870),
musical composer, lived here.

12 Seymour Street, W1

Westminster   1912

BALLANTYNE, R.M. (1825–1894),
author of books for boys, lived here.

Duneaves, Mount Park Road

Harrow   1979

BANKS, Sir Joseph (1743–1820),
President of the Royal Society; and Robert BROWN
(1773–1858) and David DON (1800–1841) botanists, lived in a
house on this site. THE LINNEAN SOCIETY met here
1820–1857.

On rebuilt premises. Replaces plaque put up in 1911 on old premises.

32 Soho Square, W1

Westminster   1938

BARBON, Nicholas
See ESSEX STREET

BARNARDO, Dr Thomas John (1845–1905),
began his work for children in a building on this site in 1866.

58 Solent House, Ben Jonson Road, E1

Tower Hamlets   1953

BARNETT, Dame Henrietta (1851–1936),
founder of Hampstead Garden Suburb; and Canon Samuel
BARNETT (1844–1913), social reformer, lived here.

Heath End House, Spaniards Road, Hampstead, NW3

Camden   1983

BARRETT, Elizabeth
See BROWNING, Elizabeth Barrett

BARRIE, Sir James (1860–1937),
novelist and dramatist, lived here.

100 Bayswater Road, W2

Westminster   1961

BARRIE, Sir James
See also ADAM, Robert

BARRY, Sir Charles (1795–1860),
architect, lived and died here.

The Elms, Clapham Common North Side, SW4

Lambeth   1950

BASEVI, George (1794–1845),
architect, lived here.

17 Savile Row, W1

Westminster   1949

BAYLIS, Lilian (1874–1937),
manager of the Old Vic and Sadlers Wells Theatres, lived
and died here.

27 Stockwell Park Road, SW9

Lambeth   1974

BAZALGETTE, Sir Joseph William (1819–1891),
civil engineer, lived here.

17 Hamilton Terrace, St. John's Wood, NW8

Westminster   1974

BEACONSFIELD, Earl of
See DISRAELI

BEARDSLEY, Aubrey (1872–1898),
artist, lived here.
114 Cambridge Street, SW1
Westminster   1948

BEATTY, David, Earl,
See COCHRANE, Thomas

BEAUCLERK, Topham
See ADELPHI TERRACE

BEAUCLERK, Lady Diana
See ADELPHI TERRACE

BEAUFORT, Sir Francis (1774–1857),
admiral and hydrographer, lived here.
51 Manchester Street, W1
Westminster   1959

BEECHAM, Sir Thomas, CH (1879–1961),
conductor and impresario, lived here.
31 Grove End Road, St. John's Wood, NW8
Westminster   1985

BEERBOHM, Sir Max (1872–1956),
artist and writer, born here.
57 Palace Gardens Terrace, W8
Kensington and Chelsea   1969

BELLOC, Hilaire (1870–1953),
poet, essayist and historian, lived here 1900–1905.
104 Cheyne Walk, SW10
Kensington and Chelsea   1973

BENEDICT, Sir Julius (1804–1885),
musical composer, lived and died here.
2 Manchester Square, W1
Westminster   1934

BENES, Dr Edward (1884–1948),
President of Czechoslovakia, lived here.
26 Gwendolen Avenue, Putney, SW15
Wandsworth   1978

BEN-GURION, David (1886–1973),
first Prime Minister of Israel, lived here.
75 Warrington Crescent, Maida Vale, W9
Westminster   1986

BENNETT, Arnold (1867–1931),
novelist, lived here.
75 Cadogan Square, SW1
Kensington and Chelsea   1958

BENTHAM, George (1800–1884),
botanist, lived here.
25 Wilton Place, Belgravia, SW1
Westminster   1978

BENTLEY, John Francis (1839–1902),
architect, lived here.
43 Old Town, Clapham, SW4
Lambeth   1950

BERLIOZ, Hector (1803–1869),
composer, stayed here in 1851.
58 Queen Anne Street, W1
Westminster   1969

BESANT, Annie (1847–1933),
social reformer, lived here in 1874.
39 Colby Road, SE19
Southwark   1963

BESANT, Sir Walter (1836–1901),
novelist and antiquary, lived and died here.
Frognal End, Frognal Gardens, Hampstead, NW3
Camden   1925

BEWDLEY, Earl Baldwin of
See BALDWIN

BIRKENHEAD, Earl of
See SMITH, F.E.

BLAKE, William
See LINNELL, John

BLAND, Dorothea
See JORDAN, Dorothy

Annie Besant *see previous page*

BLIGH, William (1754–1817),
Commander of the 'Bounty', lived here.
100 Lambeth Road, SE1
Lambeth   1952

BLUMLEIN, Alan Dower (1903–1942),
electronics engineer and inventor, lived here.
37 The Ridings, W5
Ealing   1977

BLUNT, Wilfrid Scawen
See SCAWEN-BLUNT, Wilfrid

BONAR LAW, Andrew (1858–1923),
Prime Minister, lived here.
24 Onslow Gardens, SW7
Kensington and Chelsea   1958

BOOTH, Charles (1840–1916),
pioneer in social research, lived here.
6 Grenville Place, SW7
Kensington and Chelsea   1951

BOROUGH, Stephen
See WILLOUGHBY, Sir Hugh

BOROUGH , William
See WILLOUGHBY, Sir Hugh

BORROW, George (1803–1881),
author, lived here.
22 Hereford Square, SW7
Kensington and Chelsea   1911

BOSWELL, James (1740–1795),
biographer, lived and died in a house on this site.
122 Great Portland Street, W1
Westminster   1936

BOSWELL, James
See JOHNSON, Samuel

BOW STREET
Was formed about 1637. It has been the residence of many notable men, among whom were: Henry FIELDING (1707–1754), novelist; Sir John FIELDING (d. 1780), magistrate; Grinling GIBBONS (1648–1721), wood carver; Charles MACKLIN (1697?-1797), actor; John RADCLIFFE (1650–1714), physician; Charles SACKVILLE, Earl of Dorset (1638–1706), poet; and William WYCHERLEY (1640?-1716), dramatist.

19–20 Bow Street, WC2
Westminster   1929

BRADLAUGH, Charles (1833–1891),
advocate of free thought, lived here 1870–1877.

29 Turner Street, E1
Tower Hamlets   1961

BRAILSFORD, Henry Noel (1873–1958),
writer, champion of equality and free humanity, lived here.

37 Belsize Park Gardens, NW3
Camden   1983

BRANGWYN, Sir Frank (1867–1956),
artist, lived here.

Temple Lodge, 51 Queen Caroline Street, W6
Hammersmith and Fulham   1989

BRIDGE, Frank (1879–1941),
composer and musician, lived here.

4 Bedford Gardens, W8
Kensington and Chelsea   1989

BRIDGEMAN, Charles
landscape gardener, lived here 1723–1738.

54 Broadwick Street, Soho, W1
Westminster   1984

BRIDGEMAN, Sir Orlando
See ESSEX STREET

BRIGHT, Richard (1789–1858),
physician, lived here.
11 Savile Row, W1
Westminster   1979

BROOKE, Sir Charles Vyner (1874–1963),
last Rajah of Sarawak, lived here.
13 Albion Street, W2
Westminster   1983

BROWN, Ford Madox
See MADOX BROWN, Ford

BROWN, Robert
See BANKS, Sir Joseph

BROWNING, Elizabeth Barrett (1806–1861),
poet, lived here.
99 Gloucester Place, W1
Westminster   1924

BROWNING, Elizabeth Barrett (1806–1861),
poet, lived in a house on this site 1838–1846.

Inscription in stone panel under ground floor window intended to replace RSA plaque erected in 1898 on a building now demolished. The old plaque was refixed at second floor level and reads 'Elizabeth Barrett Barrett, poetess, afterwards wife of Robert Browning lived here.'

50 Wimpole Street, W1
Westminster   1937

BRUMMELL, Beau (1778–1840),
leader of fashion, lived here.
4 Chesterfield Street, Mayfair, W1
Westminster   1984

BRUNEL, Isambard Kingdom
See 'GREAT EASTERN'

BRUNEL, Sir Marc Isambard (1769–1849),
and Isambard Kingdom BRUNEL (1806–1859), civil
engineers, lived here.

98 Cheyne Walk, SW10
Kensington and Chelsea   1954

BURGOYNE, General John (1722–1792),
lived and died here.
For another plaque at this address see SHERIDAN.

10 Hertford Street, W1
Westminster   1954

BURKE, Edmund,
author and statesman, lived here b.1729, d.1797.

37 Gerrard Street, W1
Westminster   1876

BURNE-JONES, Sir Edward
See ROSSETTI, D. G.

BURNETT, Frances Hodgson (1849–1924),
writer, lived here.

63 Portland Place, W1
Westminster   1979

BURNEY, Fanny (Madame D'Arblay),
authoress, lived here. Born 1752, died 1840.

11 Bolton Street, W1
Westminster   1885

BURNS, John (1858–1943),
statesman, lived here.

110 North Side, Clapham Common, SW4
Wandsworth   1950

BUSSON, Louis Palmella
See DU MAURIER, George

BUTT, Dame Clara (1873–1937),
singer, lived here 1901–1929.
7 Harley Road, NW3
Camden   1969

BUTTERFIELD, William (1814–1900),
architect, lived here.
42 Bedford Square, WC1
Camden   1978

CALDECOTT, Randolph (1846–1886),
artist and book illustrator, lived here.
46 Great Russell Street, WC2
Camden   1977

CAMPBELL, Colen (1676–1729),
architect and author of 'Vitruvius Britannicus', lived and
died here.
76 Brook Street, W1
Westminster   1977

CAMPBELL-BANNERMAN, Sir Henry
(1836–1908),
Prime Minister, lived here.
6 Grosvenor Place, SW1
Westminster   1959

CANAL, Antonio (CANALETTO) (1697–1768),
Venetian painter, lived here.
41 Beak Street, W1
Westminster   1925

CANNING, George (1770–1827),
statesman, lived here.
50 Berkeley Square, W1
Westminster   1979

CARLILE, Wilson, Prebendary (1847–1942),
founder of the Church Army, lived here.
34 Sheffield Terrace, W8
Kensington and Chelsea   1972

CARLYLE, Thomas (1795–1881),
essayist and historian, lived here.
33 Ampton Street, WC1
Camden   1907

CARTE, Richard D'Oyly
See ADELPHI TERRACE

CASLON, William.
The foundry established by William Caslon, typefounder (1692–1766) stood on this site 1737–1909.
21–23 Chiswell Street, EC1
Islington   1958

CASTLEREAGH, Viscount (1769–1822),
statesman, lived and died here.
Loring Hall, Water Lane, North Cray
Bexley   1989

CATO STREET CONSPIRACY
discovered here, 23 February 1820.
1a Cato Street, W1
Westminster   1977

CAVELL, Edith (1865–1915),
pioneer of modern nursing in Belgium and heroine of the Great War, trained and worked here 1896–1901.

London Hospital, Whitechapel, E1
Tower Hamlets   1988

CAVENDISH, Honble Henry,
natural philosopher, lived here, born 1731 died 1810.
Erected privately by the Duke of Bedford c.1903, adopted by the GLC in 1983.

11 Bedford Square, WC1
Camden   c.1903

CAYLEY, Sir George (1773–1857),
scientist and pioneer of aviation, lived here.

20 Hertford Street, W1
Westminster   1962

CECIL, Robert Gascoyne
See SALISBURY, 3rd Marquess of

CECIL, Viscount, of Chelwood (1864–1958),
creator of the League of Nations, lived here.

16 South Eaton Place, SW1
Westminster   1976

CHAMBERLAIN, Joseph (1836–1914),
statesman, lived here.

188 Camberwell Grove, SE5
Southwark   1920

CHAMBERLAIN, Joseph (1836–1914),
statesman, lived here.

25 Highbury Place, N5
Islington   1915

Joseph Chamberlain *see previous page*

CHAMBERLAIN, Neville (1869–1940),
Prime Minister, lived here 1923–1935.

37 Eaton Square, SW1
Westminster   1962

'CHAMPAGNE CHARLIE'
See LEYBOURNE, George

CHARLES EDWARD STUART, Prince
See ESSEX STREET

CHATHAM, Earl of
See PITT, W.

CHELSEA CHINA
was manufactured in a house at the north end of Lawrence Street 1745–1784. Tobias SMOLLETT (1721–1771), novelist, also lived in part of the house from 1750 to 1762.

16 Lawrence Street, SW3
Kensington and Chelsea   1950

CHESTERFIELD, Philip, 4th Earl of (1694–1773),
statesman and author, lived in this house.
Open to the public.

Rangers House, Chesterfield Walk, SE10
Greenwich   1937

CHESTERTON, Gilbert Keith (1874–1936),
poet, novelist and critic, lived here.

11 Warwick Gardens, W14
Kensington and Chelsea   1952

CHEVALIER, Albert (1861–1923),
music hall comedian, was born here.

17 St. Ann's Villas, W11
Kensington and Chelsea   1965

CHIPPENDALE, Thomas.
The workshop of Thomas Chippendale and his son, cabinet makers, stood near this site 1753–1813.

61 St. Martin's Lane, WC2
Westminster   1952

CHISHOLM, Caroline (1808–1877),
philanthropist, 'The Emigrants' Friend', lived here.

32 Charlton Place, N1
Islington   1983

CHOPIN, Frederic.
From this house in 1848 Frederic CHOPIN (1810–1849) went to the Guildhall to give his last public performance.

4 St. James's Place, SW1
Westminster   1981

CHURCHILL, Lord Randolph (1849–1895),
statesman, lived here 1883–1892.

2 Connaught Place, W2
Westminster   1962

CHURCHILL, Sir Winston, KG (1874–1965),
Prime Minister, lived and died here.

28 Hyde Park Gate, Kensington Gore, SW7
Kensington and Chelsea   1985

'CLAPHAM SECT'
See WILBERFORCE, William

CLARKSON, Willy (1861–1934),
theatrical wigmaker, lived and died here.

41–43 Wardour Street, W1
Westminster   1966

CLEGHORN, Elizabeth
See GASKELL, Mrs.

CLEMENS, Samuel L.
See 'TWAIN, Mark'

CLEMENTI, Muzio (1752–1832),
composer, lived here.

128 Kensington Church Street, W8
Kensington and Chelsea   1963

CLIVE of India, Lord (1725–1774),
soldier and administrator, lived here.

45 Berkeley Square, W1
Westminster   1953

COBDEN, Richard (1804–1865),
statesman, died here.

23 Suffolk Street, SW1
Westminster   1905

COBDEN-SANDERSON, Thomas James (1840–1922),
founded the Doves Bindery and Doves Press in this house, and later lived and died here.
15 Upper Mall, W6
Hammersmith and Fulham   1974

COCHRANE, Thomas, Earl of Dundonald (1775–1860),
and later David, Earl BEATTY, OM (1871–1936), admirals, lived here.
Hanover Lodge, Outer Circle, Regent's Park, NW1
Westminster   1974

COCKERELL, C.R. (Charles Robert) (1788–1863),
architect and antiquary, lived and died here.
13 Chester Terrace, NW1
Camden   1989

COLERIDGE, Samuel Taylor (1772–1834),
poet and philosopher, lived here.
7 Addison Bridge Place, W14
Hammersmith and Fulham   1950

COLERIDGE, Samuel Taylor (1772–1834),
poet and philosopher, lived here.
Plaque fixed 1905. Premises rebuilt and plaque refixed 1928. Plaque replaced by new one on same building in 1966.
71 Berners Street, W1
Westminster   1905

COLERIDGE-TAYLOR, Samuel (1875–1912),
composer of the 'Song of Hiawatha' lived here.
30 Dagnall Park, South Norwood, SE25
Croydon   1975

COLLINS, William Wilkie (1824–1889),
novelist, lived here.
65 Gloucester Place, W1
Westminster   1951

COLLINS MUSIC HALL
was here from 1862–1958.
10–11 Islington Green, N1
Islington   1968

CONAN DOYLE, Sir Arthur (1859–1930),
creator of Sherlock Holmes, lived here 1891–1894.
12 Tennison Road, South Norwood, SE25
Croydon   1973

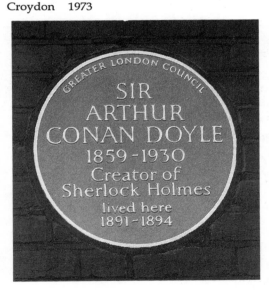

CONRAD, Joseph (1857–1924),
novelist, lived here.
17 Gillingham Street, SW1
Westminster   1984

Sir Arthur Conan Doyle

CONS, Emma (1837–1912),
philanthropist and founder of the Old Vic, lived here.
136 Seymour Place, W1
Westminster   1978

CONSTABLE, John (1776–1837),
painter, lived here.
40 Well Walk, NW3
Camden   1923

COOK, Captain James (1728–1779),
circumnavigator and explorer, lived in a house on this site.

A memorial tablet of slate erected in 1970 on the site of Cook's house with an inscription commemorating the bicentenary of his landing at Botany Bay, New South Wales.

88 Mile End Road, E1
Tower Hamlets   1970

The COUNTY HALL,
the home of London government from 1922 to 1986; LCC 1889–1965, GLC 1965–1986.

Main Entrance, County Hall, SE1
Lambeth   1986

COX, David (1783–1859),
artist, lived here.

34 Foxley Road, SW9
Lambeth   1951

CRANE, Walter (1845–1915),
artist, lived here.

13 Holland Street, W8
Kensington and Chelsea   1952

CREED, Frederick George (1871–1957),
electrical engineer, inventor of the teleprinter, lived and died
here.

20 Outram Road, Addiscombe
Croydon   1973

CRIPPS, Sir Stafford (1899–1952),
statesman, born here.

32 Elm Park Gardens, SW10
Kensington and Chelsea   1989

CROOKES, Sir William (1832–1919),
scientist, lived here from 1880 until his death.

7 Kensington Park Gardens, W11
Kensington and Chelsea   1967

CROSBY, Brass
See ESSEX STREET

CROSS, Mary Ann
See 'ELIOT, George'

CRUIKSHANK, George,
artist, lived here from 1850 to 1878 b. September 27th 1792, d.
Feb 1st 1878.

263 Hampstead Road, NW1
Camden   1885

CUBITT, Thomas (1788–1855),
master builder, lived here.

3 Lyall Street, SW1
Westminster   1959

CURZON, George Nathaniel, Marquess Curzon of Kedleston (1859–1925),
statesman, Viceroy of India, lived here.
1 Carlton House Terrace, SW1
Westminster   1976

DADD, Richard (1817–1886),
painter, lived here.
15 Suffolk Street, SW1
Westminster   1977

DALE, Sir Henry (1875–1968),
physiologist, lived here.
Mount Vernon House, Mount Vernon, Hampstead, NW3
Camden   1981

DANCE, George, the younger (1741–1825),
architect, lived and died here.
91 Gower Street, WC1
Camden   1970

D'ARBLAY, Madame
See BURNEY, Fanny

DARWIN, Charles (1809–1882),
naturalist, lived in a house on this site 1838–1842.
Biological Sciences Building, University College, (site of 110) Gower Street, WC1
Camden   1961

DAVIES, Emily (1830–1921),
founder of Girton College, Cambridge, lived here.
17 Cunningham Place, St. John's Wood, NW8
Westminster   1978

DAVIES, Thomas
See JOHNSON, Samuel

DEFOE, Daniel (1661–1731),
novelist, lived in a house on this site.
95 Stoke Newington Church Street, N16
Hackney   1932

DE GAULLE, General Charles,
President of the French National Committee, set up the
Headquarters of the Free French Forces here in 1940.
4 Carlton Gardens, SW1
Westminster   1984

DE LA RAMÉE, Maria Louisa
See 'OUIDA'

DE MORGAN, William (1839–1917),
ceramic artist and novelist, and his wife, Evelyn DE
MORGAN (1855–1919), artist, lived and died here.
127 Old Church Street, SW3
Kensington and Chelsea   1937

DE QUINCEY, Thomas (1785–1859),
wrote 'Confessions of an English Opium Eater' in this house.
36 Tavistock Street, WC2
Westminster   1981

DERBY, Earl of
See PITT, William

DICKENS, Charles (1812–1870),
novelist, lived here.
Open to the public.
48 Doughty Street, WC1
Camden   1903

DICKINSON, Goldsworthy Lowes.
This was the London home of Goldsworthy Lowes
Dickinson, author and humanist. He was born 1862 and died
1932.
Put up by private subscribers and taken over by the LCC in 1956.
11 Edwardes Square, W8
Kensington and Chelsea   1956

DILKE, Sir Charles Wentworth (1843–1911),
statesman and author, lived here.
76 Sloane Street, SW1
Kensington and Chelsea   1959

Charles Dickens

DISRAELI, Benjamin, Earl of Beaconsfield (1804–1881),
statesman, died here.
19 Curzon Street, W1
Westminster   1908

DISRAELI, Benjamin, Earl of Beaconsfield (1804–1881),
statesman, born here 1804.
First plaque put up in 1904 but removed during World War II.
22 Theobalds Road, WC1
Camden   1948

DOBSON, Henry Austin (1840–1921),
poet and essayist, lived here.
10 Redcliffe Street, SW10
Kensington and Chelsea   1959

DON, David
See BANKS, Sir Joseph

DORSET, Earl of
See BOW STREET

DOUGLAS, Norman (1868–1952),
writer, lived here.
63 Albany Mansions, Albert Bridge Road, SW11
Wandsworth   1980

D'OYLY CARTE, Richard
See ADELPHI TERRACE

DRYDEN, John,
poet, lived here, b.1631, d.1700.
43 Gerrard Street, W1
Westminster   1875

DRYSDALE, Dr Charles Vickery (1874–1961),
a founder of the Family Planning Association, opened his first birth control clinic here in 1921.

153a East Street, Walworth, SE17
Southwark   1988

DU MAURIER, George Louis Palmella Busson (1834–1896),
artist and writer, lived here 1874–1895.

Put up by private subscribers, and taken over by the LCC in 1959.

New Grove House, 28 Hampstead Grove, NW3
Camden   1900

DU MAURIER, George Louis Palmella Busson (1834–1896),
artist and writer, lived here 1863–1868.

91 Great Russell Street, WC1
Camden   1960

DU MAURIER, Sir Gerald (1873–1934),
actor manager, lived here from 1916 until his death.

Cannon Hall, 14 Cannon Place, NW3
Camden   1967

DUNDONALD, Earl
See COCHRANE, Thomas

DYSON, Sir Frank (1868–1939),
Astronomer Royal, lived here 1894–1906.

6 Vanbrugh Hill, Blackheath, SE3
Greenwich   1990

EARNSHAW, Thomas.
Site of the business premises of Thomas Earnshaw (1749–1829), noted watch and chronometer maker.

119 High Holborn, WC1
Camden   1948

EASTLAKE, Charles (1793–1865),
painter and first Director of the National Gallery, lived here.
7 Fitzroy Square, W1
Camden   1985

EDDINGTON, Sir Arthur, OM (1882–1944),
mathematician and astrophysicist lived here.
4 Bennett Park, Blackheath, SE3
Greenwich   1974

EDWARDS, John Passmore (1823–1911),
journalist, editor and builder of free public libraries, lived here.
51 Netherhall Gardens, NW3
Camden   1988

ELDON, John Scott, Lord (1751–1838),
Lord Chancellor, lived here.
6 Bedford Square, WC1
Camden   1954

ELEN, Gus (1862–1940),
music hall comedian, lived here.
3 Thurleigh Avenue, Balham, SW12
Wandsworth   1979

ELGAR, Sir Edward (1857–1934),
composer, lived here 1890–1891.
51 Avonmore Road, W14
Hammersmith and Fulham   1962

'ELIA'
See LAMB, Charles

'ELIOT, George' Mary Ann Cross (1819–1880)
novelist, lived here.
Holly Lodge, 31 Wimbledon Park Road, SW18
Wandsworth   1905

'ELIOT, George' (Mary Ann Cross, née Evans) (1819–1880),
novelist, died here.
4 Cheyne Walk, SW3
Kensington and Chelsea   1949

ELIOT, T.S., OM (1888–1965),
poet, lived and died here.
3 Kensington Court Gardens, W8
Kensington and Chelsea   1986

ELLIS, Henry Havelock (1859–1939),
pioneer in the scientific study of sex, lived here.
14 Dover Mansions, Canterbury Crescent, SW9
Lambeth   1981

ENGELS, Friedrich (1820–1895),
political philosopher, lived here 1870–1894.
121 Regent's Park Road, NW1
Camden   1972

ESSEX STREET
was laid out in the grounds of Essex House by Nicholas BARBON in 1675. Among many famous lawyers who lived here were Sir Orlando BRIDGEMAN (c.1606–1674), Lord Keeper; Henry FIELDING (1707–1754), novelist; and Brass CROSBY (1725–1793), Lord Mayor of London. James SAVAGE (1779–1852), architect had his office here. Prince CHARLES EDWARD STUART stayed at a house in the street in 1750. Rev. Theophilus LINDSEY (1723–1808), Unitarian minister, founded Essex Street Chapel here in 1774. Dr. Samuel JOHNSON established an evening club at the 'Essex Head' in 1783.

The plaque at Essex Hall, Essex Street (a modern building) commemorates the historical associations of the whole street. It was erected at 7 Essex Street in 1962 and re-erected at Essex Hall in 1964.

Essex Hall, Essex Street, WC2
Westminster   1962

ETTY, William
See PEPYS, Samuel

EVANS, Mary Ann
See ELIOT, George

EWART, William (1798–1869),
reformer, lived here.

First erected at 6 Cambridge Square, Paddington in 1952 and removed in 1962.

16 Eaton Place, SW1
Westminster   1963

FABIAN SOCIETY.
The site of 17, Osnaburgh Street where the FABIAN SOCIETY was founded in 1884.

The White House, Osnaburgh Street, NW1
Camden   1985

FARADAY, Michael,
man of science, apprentice here, b.1791, d.1867.

48 Blandford Street, W1
Westminster   1876

FAWCETT, Dame Millicent Garrett (1847–1929),
pioneer of women's suffrage, lived and died here.

2 Gower Street, WC1
Camden   1954

FERRIER, Kathleen (1912–1953),
contralto, lived here.

97 Frognal, Hampstead, NW3
Camden   1979

FIELDING, Henry (1707–1754),
novelist, lived here.

Milbourne House, Barnes Green, SW13
Richmond   1978

FIELDING, Henry
See BOW STREET

FIELDING, Henry
See ESSEX STREET

FIELDING, Sir John
See BOW STREET

FILDES, Sir Samuel Luke (1844–1927),
artist, lived here 1878–1927.

31 Melbury Road, W14
Kensington and Chelsea   1959

FISHER, Admiral of the Fleet, Lord, OM (1841–1920),
lived here as First Sea Lord 1905–1910.

16 Queen Anne's Gate, SW1
Westminster   1975

FITZROY, Admiral Robert (1805–1865),
hydrographer and meteorologist, lived here.

38 Onslow Square, SW7
Kensington and Chelsea   1981

FLAXMAN, John,
sculptor, lived and died here, b.1755, d.1826.

7 Greenwell Street, W1
Westminster   1876

FLECKER, James Elroy (1884–1915),
poet and dramatist, was born here.

9 Gilmore Road, SE13
Lewisham   1986

FLEMING, Sir Alexander (1881–1955),
discoverer of penicillin, lived here.

20a Danvers Street, SW3
Kensington and Chelsea   1981

FLEMING, Sir Ambrose (1849–1945),
scientist and electrical engineer, lived here.

9 Clifton Gardens, Maida Vale, W9
Westminster   1971

FLINDERS, Captain Matthew, RN (1774–1814),
explorer and navigator, lived here.

This plaque was removed from No.53 Stanhope Street, Camden in 1965 and re-erected at the present address in 1973.

56 Fitzroy Street, W1
Camden   1973

FLYING BOMB.
The first Flying Bomb on London fell here, 13 June 1944.

Replaces plaque erected by GLC in 1985 and subsequently stolen.

Railway Bridge, Grove Road, Bow, E3
Tower Hamlets   1988

FORBES, Vivian
See RICKETTS, Charles

FORD, Ford Madox (1873–1939),
novelist and critic, lived here.
80 Campden Hill Road, W8
Kensington and Chelsea   1973

FORESTER, C.S. (1899–1966),
novelist, lived here.
58 Underhill Road, Dulwich, SE22
Southwark   1990

FORSTER, E.M. (1879–1970),
novelist, lived here.
Arlington Park Mansions, Sutton Lane, Turnham Green, W4
Hounslow   1983

FOX, Charles James (1749–1806),
statesman, lived here.
Originally put up in 1912 on 9 Arlington Street, now demolished.
46 Clarges Street, W1
Westminster   1950

FRAMPTON, George (1860–1928),
sculptor, lived and worked here 1894–1908.
32 Queen's Grove, St. John's Wood, NW8
Westminster   1977

FRANKLIN, Benjamin (1706–1790),
American statesman and scientist, lived here.

36 Craven Street, WC2
Westminster   1914

FREAKE, Sir Charles James (1814–1884),
builder and patron of the arts, lived here.

21 Cromwell Road, SW7
Kensington and Chelsea   1981

FREUD, Sigmund (1856–1939),
founder of psychoanalysis, lived here in 1938–1939.
Open to the public.

20 Maresfield Gardens, NW3
Camden   1956

Benjamin Franklin

FRIESE-GREENE, William Edward (1855–1921),
pioneer of cinematography, lived here.

136 Maida Vale, W9
Westminster   1954

FRITH, W.P. (1819–1909),
painter, lived and died here.

114 Clifton Hill, NW8
Westminster   1973

FROBISHER, Sir Martin
See WILLOUGHBY, Sir Hugh

FROUDE, James Anthony (1818–1894),
historian and man of letters, lived here.

5 Onslow Gardens, SW7
Kensington and Chelsea   1934

FUSELI, Henry (1741–1825),
artist, lived here 1788–1803.

37 Foley Street, W1
Westminster   1961

GAINSBOROUGH, Thomas (1727–1788),
artist, lived here.

Replaces plaque put up in 1881 by RSA at No. 80.

82 Pall Mall, SW1
Westminster   1951

GAITSKELL, Hugh (1906–1963),
statesman, lived here.

18 Frognal Gardens, Hampstead, NW3
Camden   1986

GALSWORTHY, John (1867–1933),
novelist and playwright, lived here 1918–1933.

Grove Lodge, Admiral's Walk, NW3
Camden   1950

GALSWORTHY, John
See also ADAM, Robert

GALTON, Sir Francis (1822–1911),
explorer, statistician, and founder of eugenics, lived here for fifty years.
Put up privately and taken over by the LCC in 1959.
42 Rutland Gate, SW7
Westminster   1959

GANDHI, Mahatma (1869–1948),
philosopher and teacher, stayed here in 1931.
Kingsley Hall, Powis Road, E3
Tower Hamlets   1954

GANDHI, Mahatma (1869–1948),
lived here as a law student.
20 Baron's Court Road, W14
Hammersmith and Fulham   1986

GARRETT, Millicent
See FAWCETT

GARRETT ANDERSON, Elizabeth (1836–1917),
the first woman to qualify as a doctor in Britain, lived here.
20 Upper Berkeley Street, W1
Westminster   1962

GARRICK, David (1717–1779),
actor, lived here.
Garrick's Villa, Hampton Court Road
Richmond-upon-Thames   1970

GARRICK, David
See also ADELPHI TERRACE

GASKELL, Mrs Elizabeth Cleghorn (1810–1865),
novelist, born here.
93 Cheyne Walk, SW10
Kensington and Chelsea   1913

GAUDIER-BRZESKA, Henri (1891–1915),
sculptor and artist, lived here.
454 Fulham Road, SW6
Hammersmith and Fulham   1977

GERTLER, Mark (1891–1939),
painter, lived here.
32 Elder Street, E1
Tower Hamlets   1975

GIBBON, Edward (1737–1792),
historian, lived in a house on this site 1773–1783.
7 Bentinck Street, W1
Westminster   1964

GIBBONS, Grinling
See BOW STREET

GILBERT, Sir W.S. (William Schwenck) (1836–1911),
dramatist, lived here.
39 Harrington Gardens, SW7
Kensington and Chelsea   1929

GILBERT, W.S.
See SHAW, R. Norman

GISSING, George (1857–1903),
novelist, lived here 1882–1884.
33 Oakley Gardens, SW3
Kensington and Chelsea   1975

GLADSTONE, William Ewart (1809–1898),
statesman, lived here.
11 Carlton House Terrace, SW1
Westminster   1925

GLADSTONE, W.E. (William Ewart).
In a house on this site lived from 1854 to 1875 Sir Charles
LYELL (1797–1875), geologist, and from 1876–1882 W.E.
Gladstone (1809–1898), statesman.
73 Harley Street, W1
Westminster   1908

GLADSTONE, W.E.
See also PITT, William, Earl of Chatham

GLAISHER, James (1809–1903),
astronomer, meteorologist and pioneer of weather
forecasting, lived here.
20 Dartmouth Hill, SE10
Lewisham   1974

GODLEY, John Robert (1814–1861),
founder of Canterbury, New Zealand, lived and died here.
48 Gloucester Place, W1
Westminster   1951

GODWIN, George (1813–1888),
architect, journalist and social reformer, lived here.
24 Alexander Square, SW3
Kensington and Chelsea   1969

GOLDSCHMIDT, Madame
See LIND, Jenny

GOODALL, Frederick
See SHAW, R. Norman

GOSSE, Philip Henry.

Here lived Philip Henry GOSSE (1810–1888), zoologist; and Sir Edmund GOSSE (1849–1928), writer and critic, born here.

56 Mortimer Road, N1

Hackney   1983

GOUNOD, Charles (1818–1893),

composer, stayed here in 1870.

15 Morden Road, Blackheath, SE3

Greenwich   1961

GRACE, W.G. (1848–1915),

cricketer, lived here.

This plaque was originally erected at 7 Lawrie Park Road, Lewisham in 1963 and removed from there in 1964.

'Fairmount', Mottingham Lane, SE9

Bromley   1966

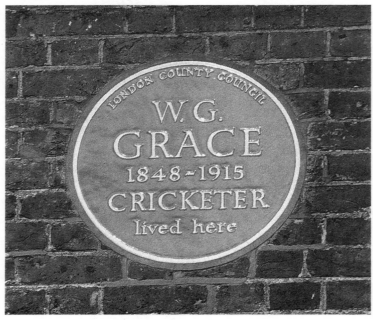

W. G. Grace

GRAHAME, Kenneth (1859–1932),
author of 'Wind in the Willows', lived here 1901–1908.
16 Phillimore Place, W8
Kensington and Chelsea   1959

GRAINGER, Percy (1882–1961),
Australian composer, folklorist and pianist, lived here.
31 King's Road, Chelsea, SW3
Kensington and Chelsea   1988

GRAY, Henry (1827–1861),
anatomist, lived here.
8 Wilton Street, SW1
Westminster   1947

'GREAT EASTERN', The.

Launched 1858. Largest steamship of the century, was built here by I.K. (Isambard Kingdom) BRUNEL (1806–1859), civil engineer and J. (John) Scott RUSSELL (1808–1882), naval architect.

Removed prior to demolition 1974, to be re-erected when redevelopment completed.

Westferry Road, E14

Tower Hamlets   1954

GREATER LONDON COUNCIL

See COUNTY HALL

GREAVES, Walter (1846–1930),

artist, lived here 1855–1897.

104 Cheyne Walk, SW10

Kensington and Chelsea   1973

GREEN, John Richard (1837–1883),

historian of the English people, lived here.

Plaque fixed 1909. Premises rebuilt and plaque refixed, 1925. Plaque replaced by new one on same building in 1964.

4 Beaumont Street, W1

Westminster   1909

GREEN, John Richard (1837–1883),

historian of the English people, lived here 1866–1869.

St. Philip's Vicarage, Newark Street, E1

Tower Hamlets   1910

GREENAWAY, Kate (1846–1901),

artist, lived and died here.

39 Frognal, NW3

Camden   1949

GREET, Sir Philip Ben (1857–1936),

actor-manager, lived here 1920–1936.

160 Lambeth Road, SE1

Lambeth   1961

GREY, Sir Edward, Viscount Grey of Falloden (1862–1933),
Foreign Secretary, lived here.
3 Queen Anne's Gate, SW1
Westminster   1981

GRIMALDI, Joseph (1778–1837),
clown, lived here 1818–1828.
56 Exmouth Market, EC1
Islington   1989

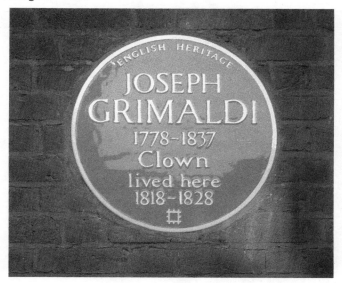

GROSER, Reverend St. John (1890–1966),
priest and social reformer, lived here.
Royal Foundation of St. Katherine, 2 Butcher Row, E14
Tower Hamlets   1990

Joseph Grimaldi *see previous page*

GROSSMITH, George, Senior (1847–1912),
actor and author, lived here.
28 Dorset Square, NW1
Westminster   1963

GROSSMITH, George, Junior (1874–1935),
actor-manager, lived here.
3 Spanish Place, W1
Westminster   1963

GROTE, George (1794–1871),
historian, died here.
12 Savile Row, W1
Westminster   1905

HAGGARD, Sir Henry Rider (1856–1925),
novelist, lived here 1885–1888.
69 Gunterstone Road, W14
Hammersmith and Fulham   1977

HALDANE, Lord (1856–1928),
statesman, lawyer and philosopher, lived here.
28 Queen Anne's Gate, SW1
Westminster   1954

HALLAM, Henry (1777–1859),
historian, lived here.
67 Wimpole Street, W1
Westminster   1904

HAMMOND, J.L. and Barbara,
social historians, lived here 1906–1913.
'Hollycot', Vale of Health, Hampstead, NW3
Camden   1972

HANDEL, George Frederick (1685–1759),
musician, lived and died here.
Replaces plaque put up in 1875 by RSA.
25 Brook Street, W1
Westminster   1952

HANDLEY, Tommy (1892–1949),
radio comedian, lived here.
34 Craven Road, Paddington, W2
Westminster   1980

HANSOM, Joseph Aloysius (1803–1882),
architect, founder editor of 'The Builder' and inventor of the
Hansom Cab, lived here.
27 Sumner Place, SW7
Kensington and Chelsea   1980

HARDY, Thomas (1840–1928),
poet and novelist, lived here 1878–1881.
Plaque replaced by new one on same building in 1962.
172 Trinity Road, Tooting, SW17
Wandsworth   1940

HARDY, Thomas
See also ADELPHI TERRACE

HARLEY, Robert
See PEPYS, Samuel

HARMSWORTH, Alfred, Viscount Northcliffe (1865–1922),
journalist and newspaper proprietor, lived here.
31 Pandora Road, West Hampstead, NW6
Camden   1979

HARRISON, John (1693–1776),
inventor of the marine chronometer, lived and died in a
house on this site.
Summit House, Red Lion Square, WC1
Camden   1954

HARTE, Francis Bret (1836–1902),
American writer, lived here.
74 Lancaster Gate, W2
Westminster   1977

HAWKINS, Sir Anthony Hope (Anthony Hope) (1863–1933),
novelist, lived here 1903–1917.
41 Bedford Square, WC1
Camden   1976

HAWTHORNE, Nathaniel (1804–1864),
American author, stayed here in 1856.
4 Pond Road, Blackheath, SE3
Greenwich   1953

HAYDON, Benjamin Robert (1786–1846),
painter, and John Charles Felix ROSSI, (1762–1839), sculptor, lived here.
116 Lisson Grove, NW1
Westminster   1959

HAZLITT, William (1778–1830),
essayist, died here.
6 Frith Street, W1
Westminster   1905

HEATH ROBINSON, W. (1872–1944),
illustrator and comic artist, lived here.
75 Moss Lane, Pinner
Harrow   1976

HEINE, Heinrich (1799–1856),
German poet and essayist, lived here 1827.
32 Craven Street, WC2
Westminster   1912

HENDERSON, Arthur (1863–1935),
statesman, lived here.
13 Rodenhurst Road, Clapham, SW4
Lambeth   1980

HENTY, G.A. (George Alfred) (1832–1902),
author, lived here.
33 Lavender Gardens, SW11
Wandsworth   1953

HERFORD, Robert Travers (1860–1950),
Unitarian minister, scholar, and interpreter of Judaism, lived
and worked here.
Open to the public.
Dr Williams's Library, 14 Gordon Square, WC1
Camden   1990

HERZEN, Alexander (1812–1870),
Russian political thinker, lived here 1860–1863.
1 Orsett Terrace, W2
Westminster   1970

HESELTINE, Philip Arnold
See WARLOCK, Peter

HESS, Dame Myra (1890–1965),
pianist, lived here.
48 Wildwood Road, NW11
Barnet   1987

HILL, Sir Rowland (1795–1879),
postal reformer, lived here.
1 Orme Square, W2
Westminster   1907

HILL, Sir Rowland, KCB,

originator of the Penny Post, lived here 1849–1879. Born 1795. Died 1879.

The above plaque was first erected by the Royal Society of Arts in 1892 and moved to its present location in May 1978.

Royal Free Hospital, Pond Street, Hampstead, NW3

Camden   1978

HOBBS, Jack (1882–1963),

cricketer, lived here.

17 Englewood Road, SW12

Lambeth   1986

HODGKIN, Thomas (1798–1866),

physician, reformer and philanthropist, lived here.

35 Bedford Square, WC1

Camden   1985

HOGG, Quintin (1845–1903),

founder of the Polytechnic, Regent Street, lived here 1885–1898.

5 Cavendish Square, W1

Westminster   1965

HOLMAN-HUNT, William, OM (1827–1910),

painter, lived and died here.

18 Melbury Road, W14

Kensington and Chelsea   1923

HOOD, Thomas (1799–1845),

poet, died here.

Devonshire Lodge, 28 Finchley Road, NW8

Westminster   1912

HOOD, Thomas

See also ADAM, Robert

HOPKINS, Gerard Manley (1844–1889),
poet, lived and studied in Manresa House.

Gatepost at Manresa House, Holybourne Avenue, Roehampton, SW15

Wandsworth   1979

HORE-BELISHA, Lord (1893–1957),
statesman, lived here.

16 Stafford Place, SW1

Westminster   1980

HORNIMAN, John (1803–1893)
and Frederick John HORNIMAN (1835–1906), tea merchants, collectors and public benefactors, lived here.

Coombe Cliff Centre, Coombe Road, Croydon

Croydon   1988

HORNIMAN MUSEUM and GARDENS, The
were given to the people of London in 1901 by Frederick John HORNIMAN, who lived near this site.

The Horniman Museum, London Road, SE23

Lewisham   1985

HOUSMAN, A.E. (1859–1936),
poet and scholar, wrote 'A Shropshire Lad' while living here.

17 North Road, Highgate, N6

Haringey   1969

HOWARD, John (1726?–1790),
prison reformer, lived here.

23 Great Ormond Street, WC1

Camden   1908

HUDSON, W.H. (William Henry)
with view of 'The house where I was born in the South
American Pampas . . .' Hudson's friends' Society of Quilmes,
near Buenos Aires, where the great writer was born on August
4th 1841, and where he spent his youth, has placed this bronze
plaque at 40 St. Luke's Road, London, the house in which
Hudson lived his last years, and died on August 18th, 1922.

40 St. Luke's Road, W11
Kensington and Chelsea   1938

HUGHES, Hugh Price (1847–1902),
Methodist preacher, lived and died here.

8 Taviton Street, WC1
Camden   1989

HUGHES, Mary (1860–1941),
friend of all in need, lived and worked here 1926–1941.

71 Vallance Road, E2
Tower Hamlets   1961

HUNT, James Henry, Leigh (1784–1859),
essayist and poet, lived here.

22 Upper Cheyne Row, SW3
Kensington and Chelsea   1905

HUNTER, John (1728–1793),
surgeon, lived here.
Plaque fixed, 1907. Premises rebuilt and plaque refixed 1931.

31 Golden Square, W1
Westminster   1907

HUNTER, William.
This was the home and museum of Dr. William Hunter,
anatomist (1718–1783).

Lyric Theatre (rear portion), Great Windmill Street, W1
Westminster   1952

HUSKISSON, William (1770–1830),
statesman, lived here.
28 St. James's Place, SW1
Westminster 1962

HUTCHINSON, Sir Jonathan (1828–1913),
surgeon, scientist and teacher, lived here.
15 Cavendish Square, W1
Westminster 1981

HUTCHISON, Ronald MacDonald
See TATE, Harry

HUXLEY, Thomas Henry (1825–1895),
biologist, lived here.
38 Marlborough Place, NW8
Westminster 1910

HYNDMAN, Henry Mayers (1842–1921),
socialist leader, lived and died here.
13 Well Walk, NW3
Camden 1972

INNER LONDON EDUCATION AUTHORITY.
The home of Inner London's Education Service from 1922; ILEA succeeding the London School Board (1870–1904) and the LCC (1904–1965).
Main Entrance, County Hall, SE1
Lambeth 1986

INNES, John (1829–1904),
founder of the John Innes Horticultural Institute, lived here.
Manor House, Watery Lane, SW20
Merton 1978

IRVING, Edward (1792–1834),
founder of the Catholic Apostolic church, lived here.
4 Claremont Square, Islington, N1
Islington   1982

IRVING, Sir Henry (1838–1905),
actor, lived here 1872–1899.
15a Grafton Street, W1
Westminster   1950

IRVING, Washington (1783–1859),
American writer, lived here.
8 Argyll Street, W1
Westminster   1983

ISAACS, Rufus, 1st Marquess of Reading (1860–1935),
lawyer and statesman, lived and died here.
32 Curzon Street, W1
Westminster   1971

JACKSON, John Hughlings (1835–1911),
physician, lived here.
3 Manchester Square, W1
Westminster   1932

JAMES, Henry (1843–1916),
writer, lived here 1886–1902.
34 De Vere Gardens, W8
Kensington and Chelsea   1949

JEFFERIES, Richard (1848–1887),
naturalist and writer, lived here.
59 Footscray Road, Eltham, SE29
Greenwich   1986

JELLICOE, Admiral of the Fleet, Earl, OM (1859–1935),
lived here.

25 Draycott Place, SW3
Kensington and Chelsea   1975

JEROME, Jerome K. (1859–1927),
author, wrote 'Three Men in a Boat' while living here at Flat 104.

91–104 Chelsea Gardens, Chelsea Bridge Road, SW1
Westminster   1989

JINNAH, Mohammed Ali (Quaid i Azam) (1876–1948),
founder of Pakistan, stayed here in 1895.

35 Russell Road, W14
Kensington and Chelsea   1955

Jerome K. Jerome

JOHN, Augustus.
This house was built for AUGUSTUS JOHN (1878–1961), painter.
28 Mallord Street, SW3
Kensington and Chelsea   1981

JOHNSON, Amy (1903–1941),
aviator, lived here.
Vernon Court, Hendon Way, NW2
Barnet   1987

JOHNSON, Samuel (1709-1784),
In this house, occupied by Thomas DAVIES, bookseller, Dr. Samuel JOHNSON first met James BOSWELL in 1763.

8 Russell Street, Covent Garden, WC2
Westminster   1984

JOHNSON, Dr Samuel
See ESSEX STREET

JOHNSTON, Edward (1872-1944),
master calligrapher, lived here 1905-1912.

3 Hammersmith Terrace, W6
Hammersmith and Fulham   1977

JONES, Dr Ernest (1879-1958),
pioneer psychoanalyst, lived here.

19 York Terrace East, Regents Park, NW1
Westminster   1985

JORDAN, Mrs Dorothy (née Bland) (1762-1816),
actress, lived here.

30 Cadogan Place, SW1
Kensington and Chelsea   1975

KARSAVINA, Tamara (1885-1978),
ballerina, lived here.

108 Frognal, NW3
Camden   1987

KEATS, John,

poet, lived in this house, b.1795, d.1821.
Open to the public.

'Keats' House' (Wentworth Place), Keats Grove, Hampstead, NW3

Camden   1896

KEDLESTON, Marquess of

See CURZON, George Nathaniel

KEYNES, John Maynard (1883–1946),

economist, lived here 1916–1946.

46 Gordon Square, Bloomsbury, WC1

Camden   1975

KINGSLEY, Charles (1819–1875),

writer, lived here.

56 Old Church Street, Chelsea, SW3

Kensington and Chelsea   1979

John Keats *see previous page*

KINGSLEY, Mary (1862–1900),
traveller and ethnologist, lived here as a child.

22 Southwood Lane, N6
Haringey   1975

KIPLING, Rudyard (1865–1936),
poet and story writer, lived here 1889–1891.
Replaces plaque put up in 1940.

43 Villiers Street, WC2
Westminster   1957

KITCHENER of Khartoum, Field Marshal Earl, KG (1850–1916),
lived here 1914–1915.
2 Carlton Gardens, SW1
Westminster   1924

KLEIN, Melanie (1882–1960),
psychoanalyst and pioneer of child analysis, lived here.
42 Clifton Hill, NW8
Westminster   1985

KNEE, Fred (1868–1914),
London Labour Party pioneer and housing reformer, lived here.
24 Sugden Road, SW11
Wandsworth   1986

KNIGHT, Dame Laura (1877–1970)
and Harold KNIGHT (1874–1961), painters, lived here.
16 Langford Place, St. John's Wood, NW8
Westminster   1983

KOKOSCHKA, Oskar (1886–1980),
painter, lived here.
Eyre Court, Finchley Road, NW8
Westminster   1986

KOSSUTH, Louis (1802–1894),
Hungarian patriot, stayed here.
39 Chepstow Villas, W11
Kensington and Chelsea   1959

KROPOTKIN, Prince Peter (1842–1921),
theorist of anarchism, lived here.
6 Crescent Road
Bromley   1989

LABOUR PARTY
Site of the Congregational Memorial Hall; The LABOUR
PARTY was founded here, 27th February 1900.

Caroone House, Farringdon Street, EC4
City   1985

LAMB, Charles 'Elia' (1775–1834),
essayist, lived here.

64 Duncan Terrace, N1
Islington   1907

LANG, Andrew (1844–1912),
man of letters, lived here in 1876–1912.

1 Marloes Road, W8
Kensington and Chelsea   1959

LANGTRY, Lillie (1852–1929),
actress, lived here.
Cadogan Hotel, 21 Pont Street, SW1
Kensington and Chelsea   1980

LASKI, Harold (1893–1950),
teacher and political philosopher, lived here 1926–1950.
5 Addison Bridge Place, W14
Hammersmith and Fulham   1974

LAUDER, Sir Harry (1870–1950),
music hall artist, lived here 1903–1911.
46 Longley Road, Tooting, SW17
Wandsworth   1969

LAVERY, Sir John (1856–1941),
painter, lived here 1899–1940.
5 Cromwell Place, SW7
Kensington and Chelsea   1966

LAWRENCE, David Herbert (1885–1930),
novelist and poet, lived here in 1915.
1 Byron Villas, Vale of Health, Hampstead, NW3
Camden   1969

LAWRENCE, Susan (1871–1947),
social reformer, lived here.
44 Westbourne Terrace, W2
Westminster   1987

LAWRENCE, T.E. (1888–1935),
'Lawrence of Arabia' lived here.
14 Barton Street, SW1
Westminster   1966

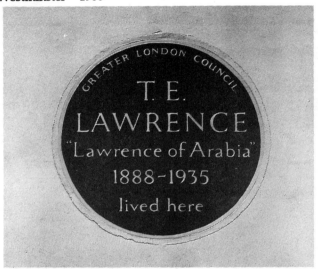

LEAR, Edward (1812–1888),
artist and writer, lived here.
30 Seymour Street, W1
Westminster   1960

LECKY, W.E.H. (William Edward Hartpole) (1838–1903),
historian and essayist, lived and died here.
38 Onslow Gardens, SW7
Kensington and Chelsea   1955

LEIGHTON, Frederick, Lord (1830–1896),
painter, lived and died here.
Open to the public.
Leighton House, 12 Holland Park Road, W14
Kensington and Chelsea   1958

T.E. Lawrence

LENO, Dan (1860–1904),
music hall comedian, lived here 1898–1901.
56 Akerman Road, SW9
Lambeth   1962

LETHABY, William Richard (1857–1931),
architect and first principal of this school in 1896 to 1911.
Central School of Arts and Crafts, Southampton Row, WC1
Camden   1957

LETHABY, William Richard (1857–1931),
architect, lived here 1880–1891.
20 Calthorpe Street, WC1
Camden   1979

LEWIS, Percy Wyndham (1882–1957),
painter, lived here.
61 Palace Gardens Terrace, W8
Kensington and Chelsea   1983

LEYBOURNE, George (1842–1884),
music hall comedian 'Champagne Charlie', lived and died here.
136 Englefield Road, N1
Islington   1970

LIND, Jenny (Madame Goldschmidt) (1820–1887),
singer, lived here.
189 Old Brompton Road, SW7
Kensington and Chelsea   1909

LINDSEY, Rev. Theophilus
See ESSEX STREET

LINNEAN SOCIETY
See BANKS, Sir Joseph

LINNELL, John (1792–1882),
painter, lived here. BLAKE, William (1757–1827), poet and
artist, stayed here as his guest.
'Old Wyldes', North End, Hampstead, NW3
Barnet   1975

LISTER, Joseph, Lord (1827–1912),
surgeon, lived here.
12 Park Crescent, W1
Westminster   1915

'LITTLE TICH'
See RELPH, Harry

LLOYD GEORGE, David (1865–1945),
Prime Minister, lived here.
3 Routh Road, SW18
Wandsworth   1967

LLOYD, Marie (1870–1922),
music hall artiste, lived here.
55 Graham Road, E8
Hackney   1977

LONDON COUNTY COUNCIL
See COUNTY HALL

LOUDON, John Claudius.
Here lived John and Jane Loudon (1783–1843), and
(1807–1858). Their horticultural work gave new beauty to
London squares.
3 Porchester Terrace, W2
Westminster   1953

LUBBOCK, Sir John
See AVEBURY, Baron

Marie Lloyd *see previous page*

LUCAN, Arthur (Arthur Towle) (1887–1954),
entertainer and creator of Old Mother Riley, lived here.

11 Forty Lane, Wembley
Brent   1978

LUGARD, Lord (1858–1945),
colonial administrator, lived here 1912–1919.

51 Rutland Gate, Hyde Park, SW7
Westminster   1972

LUTYENS, Sir Edwin Landseer
See PEARSON, J.L.

LYELL, Sir Charles
See GLADSTONE, W.E.

MACAULAY, Thomas Babington, Lord (1800–1859),
historian and man of letters, lived here.

This tablet was first erected by the London County Council in 1903 on Holly Lodge which stood on this site. It was re-erected here in 1969.

Holly Lodge (now Atkins Buildings, Queen Elizabeth College), Campden Hill, W8
Kensington and Chelsea   1903

MACAULAY, Zachary (1768–1838),
philanthropist, and his son, Thomas Babington MACAULAY, afterwards Lord Macaulay (1800–1859) historian and man of letters, lived here.

5 The Pavement, Clapham Common, SW4
Lambeth   1930

MACDONALD, Ramsay (1866–1937),
Prime Minister, lived here 1916–1925.

9 Howitt Road, NW3
Camden   1963

McGILL, Donald (1875–1962),
postcard cartoonist, lived here.

5 Bennett Park, Blackheath, SE3
Greenwich   1977

MACKLIN, Charles
See BOW STREET

The Rachel McMILLAN College (1930–1977);
Margaret McMILLAN, CH (1860–1931), pioneer of nursery
education, lived here.

Creek Road, Deptford, SE8
Greenwich   1985

MADOX BROWN, Ford (1821–1893),
painter, lived here.

56 Fortess Road, Kentish Town, NW5
Camden   1976

MALLARME, Stephane (1842–1898),
poet, stayed here in 1863.

6 Brompton Square, SW3
Kensington and Chelsea   1959

MALLON, Dr Jimmy, CH (1874–1961),
warden of Toynbee Hall, champion of social reform, lived here.

Toynbee Hall, Commercial Street, E1
Tower Hamlets   1984

MALONE, Edmond (1741–1812),
Shakespearian scholar, lived here 1779–1812.

40 Langham Street, W1
Westminster   1962

MANBY, Charles (1804–1884),
civil engineer, lived here.

60 Westbourne Terrace, W2
Westminster   1961

MANNING, Cardinal Henry Edward (1808–1892),
lived here.
22 Carlisle Place, SW1
Westminster   1914

MANSBRIDGE, Albert (1876–1952),
founder of the Workers' Educational Association, lived here.
198 Windsor Road, Ilford
Redbridge   1967

MANSFIELD, Katherine (1888–1923),
writer, and her husband, John Middleton MURRY (1889–1957), critic, lived here.
17 East Heath Road, NW3
Camden   1969

MANSON, Sir Patrick (1844–1922),
father of modern tropical medicine, lived here.
50 Welbeck Street, W1
Westminster   1985

MARCONI, Guglielmo (1874–1937),
the pioneer of wireless communication, lived here in 1896–1897.
Replaces plaque put up in 1952.
71 Hereford Road, W2
Westminster   1954

MARRYAT Captain Frederick (1792–1848),
novelist, lived here.
3 Spanish Place, W1
Westminster   1953

MARSDEN, William (1796–1867),
surgeon, founder of the Royal Free and Royal Marsden Hospitals, lived here.
65 Lincoln's Inn Fields, WC2
Camden   1986

MARX, Karl (1818–1883),
lived here 1851–1856.
28 Dean Street, W1
Westminster   1967

MATTHAY, Tobias (1858–1945),
teacher and pianist, lived here.
21 Arkwright Road, NW3
Camden   1979

MAUGHAM, William Somerset (1874–1965),
novelist and playwright, lived here 1911–1919.
6 Chesterfield Street, W1
Westminster   1975

MAURICE, Frederick Denison (1805–1872),
Christian philosopher and educationalist, lived here
1862–1866.
2 Upper Harley Street, NW1
Westminster   1977

MAXIM, Sir Hiram (1840–1896),
inventor and engineer, designed and manufactured THE
MAXIM GUN in a workshop on these premises.
57d Hatton Garden, EC1
Camden   1966

MAXWELL, James Clerk (1831–1879),
physicist, lived here.
16 Palace Gardens Terrace, W8
Kensington and Chelsea   1923

MAY, Phil (1864–1903),
artist, lived and worked here.
20 Holland Park Road, W14
Kensington and Chelsea   1982

MAYHEW, Henry (1812–1887),
founder of 'Punch' and author of 'London Labour and the
London Poor', lived here.
55 Albany Street, NW1
Camden   1953

MAZZINI, Giuseppe (1805–1872),
Italian patriot, lived here.
183 Gower Street, NW1
Camden   1950

MEREDITH, George, OM (1828–1909),
poet and novelist, lived here.
7 Hobury Street, SW10
Kensington and Chelsea   1976

METTERNICH, Prince (1773–1859),
Austrian statesman, lived here in 1848.
44 Eaton Square, SW1
Westminster   1970

MEYNELL, Alice (1847–1922),
poet and essayist, lived here.
47 Palace Court, W2
Westminster   1948

MILL, John Stuart (1806–1873),
philosopher, lived here.
18 Kensington Square, W8
Kensington and Chelsea   1907

MILLAIS, Sir John Everett, Bt PRA (1829–1896),
painter, lived and died here.
2 Palace Gate, W8
Kensington and Chelsea   1926

MILLBANK PRISON.
Near this site stood Millbank Prison, which was opened in 1816 and closed in 1890. This buttress stood at the head of the river steps from which, until 1867, prisoners sentenced to transportation embarked on their journey to Australia.

Millbank, SW1
Westminster   1965

MILNE, A.A. (1882–1956),
author, lived here.

13 Mallord Street, SW3
Kensington and Chelsea   1979

MILNER, Alfred, Lord (1854–1925),
statesman, lived here.

14 Manchester Square, W1
Westminster   1967

MONDRIAN, Piet Cornelis (1872–1944),
painter, lived here.

60 Parkhill Road, NW3
Camden   1975

MONTEFIORE, Sir Moses (1784–1885),
philanthropist and Jewish leader, lived here for sixty years.

99 Park Lane, W1
Westminster   1984

MONTGOMERY, Field Marshal, Viscount, of Alamein (1887–1976),
was born here.

Oval House, 52–54 Kennington Oval, SE11
Lambeth   1987

MOORE, George (1852–1933),
author, lived and died here.

121 Ebury Street, SW1
Westminster   1936

MOORE, Tom (1779–1852),
Irish poet, lived here.

This plaque was removed from 28 Bury Street, St. James's Westminster in 1962.

85 George Street, W1
Westminster   1963

MORRELL, Lady Ottoline (1873–1938),
literary hostess and patron of the Arts, lived here.

10 Gower Street, WC1
Westminster   1984

MORRIS, William
See ROSSETTI

MORRIS, William
See also RED HOUSE

MORRISON, Herbert, Lord Morrison of Lambeth (1888–1965),
Cabinet Minister and leader of the London County Council, lived here 1929–1960.

55 Archery Road, Eltham, SE9
Greenwich   1977

MORSE, Samuel (1791–1872),
American painter and inventor of the Morse Code, lived here 1812–1815.

141 Cleveland Street, W1
Westminster   1962

MOZART, Wolfgang Amadeus (1756–1791),
composed his first symphony here in 1764.

180 Ebury Street, SW1
Westminster   1939

MUIRHEAD, Alexander (1848–1920),
electrical engineer, lived here.
20 Church Road, Shortlands
Bromley   1981

MURRY, John Middleton
See MANSFIELD, Katherine

NAPOLEON III (1808–1873),
Emperor of the French, lived here 1848.
1c King Street, St. James's, SW1
Westminster   1875

NEHRU, Jawaharlal (1889–1964),
first Prime Minister of India, lived here in 1910 and 1912.
60 Elgin Crescent, W11
Kensington and Chelsea   1989

NELSON
lived here in 1797. Born 1758, fell at Trafalgar 1805.
147 New Bond Street (site), W1
Westminster   1876

NELSON, Horatio, Lord (1758–1805),
lived here in 1798.
103 New Bond Street, W1
Westminster   1958

NEWMAN, John Henry.
In this house John Henry NEWMAN (1801–1890), later
Cardinal Newman, spent some of his early years.
Grey Court, Ham Street, Ham
Richmond   1981

NEWTON, Sir Isaac (1642–1727),
natural philosopher, lived here.

Plaque fixed 1908. Premises rebuilt and plaque refixed, 1915.

87 Jermyn Street, SW1

Westminster   1908

NIGHTINGALE, Florence (1820–1910),
lived and died in a house on this site.

New plaque on rebuilt premises. Original plaque erected by the Duke of Westminster and removed when the house was pulled down in 1929.

10 South Street, W1

Westminster   1955

NOLLEKENS, Joseph (1737–1823),
sculptor, lived and died in a house on this site.

44 Mortimer Street, W1

Westminster   1954

NORTHCLIFFE, Viscount
See HARMSWORTH, Alfred

NOVELLO, Ivor (1893–1951),
composer and actor-manager, lived and died in a flat on the top floor of this building.

11 Aldwych, WC2

Westminster   1973

OATES, Captain Lawrence (1880–1912),
Antarctic explorer, lived here.

309 Upper Richmond Road, SW15

Wandsworth   1973

OLIVER, Percy Lane (1878–1944),
founder of the first voluntary blood donor service, lived and worked here.

5 Colyton Road, SE22

Southwark   1979

ONSLOW, Arthur (1691–1768),
Speaker of the House of Commons from 1728 to 1761, lived in a house on this site.

Replaces plaque put up in 1912 on building now demolished.

20 Soho Square, W1

Westminster   1927

ORFORD, Earl of
See WALPOLE, Sir Robert

ORPEN, Sir William (1878–1931),
painter, lived here.

8 South Bolton Gardens, SW5

Kensington and Chelsea   1978

ORWELL, George (1903–1950),
novelist and political essayist, lived here.

50 Lawford Road, NW5

Camden   1980

'OUIDA' (Maria Louisa de la Ramée) (1839–1908),
novelist, lived here.

11 Ravenscourt Square, W6

Hammersmith and Fulham   1952

OXFORD and ASQUITH, 1st Earl of
See ASQUITH

OXFORD, Earl of
See PEPYS, Samuel

PALGRAVE, Francis Turner (1824–1897),
compiler of 'The Golden Treasury', lived here 1862–1875.

5 York Gate, Regent's Park, NW1

Westminster   1976

PALMER, Samuel (1805–1881),
artist, lived here 1851–1861.

6 Douro Place, W8
Kensington and Chelsea   1972

PALMERSTON, Henry John Temple, 3rd Viscount (1784–1865),
statesman, lived here.

Plaque fixed 1907. Premises rebuilt 1933. Plaque refixed 1936.

4 Carlton Gardens, SW1
Westminster   1907

PALMERSTON, Henry John Temple, 3rd Viscount (1784–1865),
Prime Minister, born here.

20 Queen Anne's Gate, SW1
Westminster   1925

PALMERSTON, Lord (1784–1865).
In this house formerly a Royal residence lived Lord Palmerston, Prime Minister and Foreign Secretary.

Naval and Military Club, 94 Piccadilly, W1
Westminster   1961

PANKHURST, Sylvia (1882–1960),
campaigner for women's rights, lived here.

120 Cheyne Walk, SW10
Kensington and Chelsea   1985

PARRY, Sir Charles Hubert (1848–1918),
musician, lived here.

17 Kensington Square, W8
Kensington and Chelsea   1949

PASSMORE EDWARDS
See EDWARDS, John Passmore

PATEL, Sardar (1875–1950),
Indian statesman, lived here.
23 Aldridge Road Villas, W11
Westminster   1986

PATMORE, Coventry (1823–1896),
poet and essayist, lived here 1863–1864.
14 Percy Street, W1
Camden   1960

PEABODY, George (1795–1869),
philanthropist, died here.
80 Eaton Square, SW1
Westminster   1976

PEARSON, John Loughborough (1817–1897),
and later Sir Edwin Landseer LUTYENS (1869–1944),
architects, lived and died here.
13 Mansfield Street, W1
Westminster   1962

PEARSON, Karl (1857–1936),
pioneer statistician, lived here.
7 Well Road, Hampstead, NW3
Camden   1983

PEEL, Sir Robert (1750–1830),
manufacturer and reformer, and his son, Sir Robert PEEL
(1788–1850), Prime Minister, founder of the Metropolitan
Police, lived here.
16 Upper Grosvenor Street, W1
Westminster   1988

PEPYS, Samuel (1633–1703),
diarist and Secretary of the Admiralty, lived here 1679–1688.
12 Buckingham Street, WC2
Westminster   1947

PEPYS, Samuel.

In a house formerly standing on this site lived Samuel PEPYS (1633–1703), diarist and Robert HARLEY, Earl of Oxford (1661–1724), statesman; and in this house lived William ETTY (1787–1849), painter, and Clarkson STANFIELD (1793–1867), painter.

14 Buckingham Street, WC2

Westminster   1908

PERCEVAL, The Hon. Spencer (1762–1812),
Prime Minister, lived here.

59–60 Lincoln's Inn Fields, WC2

Camden   1914

PETRIE, Sir William Matthew Flinders (1853–1942),
Egyptologist, lived here.

5 Cannon Place, NW3

Camden   1954

PHELPS, Samuel (1804–1878),
tragedian, lived here.

8 Canonbury Square, N1

Islington   1911

PHILPOT, Glyn
See RICKETTS, Charles

PICK, Frank (1878–1941),
pioneer of good design for London Transport, lived here.

15 Wildwood Road, NW11

Barnet   1981

PINERO, Sir Arthur (1855–1934),
playwright, lived here 1909–1934.

115a Harley Street, W1

Westminster   1970

PISSARRO, Lucien (1863–1944),
painter, printer, wood engraver, lived here.

27 Stamford Brook Road, Chiswick, W6
Hammersmith and Fulham   1976

PITT, William, Earl of Chatham.
Here lived three Prime Ministers: William PITT, Earl of
Chatham (1708–1778); Edward Geoffrey STANLEY, Earl of
Derby (1799–1869); William Ewart GLADSTONE (1809–1898).

10 St. James's Square, SW1
Westminster   1910

PITT, William, the younger (1759–1806),
Prime Minister, lived here 1803 to 1804.
Replaces first plaque put up in 1904 and later removed.

120 Baker Street, W1
Westminster   1949

PITT-RIVERS, Lieutenant General Augustus Henry Lane Fox (1827–1900),
anthropologist and archaeologist, lived here.

4 Grosvenor Gardens, SW1
Westminster   1983

PLAATJE, Sol (1876–1932),
black South African writer, lived here.

25 Carnarvon Road, E10
Waltham Forest   1986

PLACE, Francis (1771–1854),
political reformer, lived here 1833–1851.

21 Brompton Square, SW3
Kensington and Chelsea   1961

PLAYFAIR, Sir Nigel (1874–1934),
actor-manager, lived here.

26 Pelham Crescent, SW7
Kensington and Chelsea   1965

PORTUGUESE EMBASSY.
These two houses were the Portuguese Embassy (1724–1747). The MARQUESS OF POMBAL, ambassador 1739–1744, lived here.
23–24 Golden Square, W1
Westminster   1980

PRIESTLEY, Joseph (1733–1804),
scientist, philosopher and theologian, was Minister to the Gravel Pit Meeting here in 1793–1794.
Ram Place, E9
Hackney   1985

PRIORY of St. John the Baptist, Holywell, and The THEATRE.
The site of this building forms part of what was once the precinct of the Priory of St. John the Baptist, Holywell. Within a few yards stood from 1577 to 1598 the first London building specially devoted to the performance of plays and known as 'The Theatre'.
86–88 Curtain Road, EC2
Hackney   1920

PRYDE, James
See RICKETTS, Charles

QUAID I AZAM
See JINNAH

RACKHAM, Arthur (1867–1939),
illustrator, lived here.
16 Chalcot Gardens, NW3
Camden   1981

RADCLIFFE, John
See BOW STREET

RAGLAN, Lord Fitzroy Somerset, 1st Baron (1788–1855),
commander during the Crimean War, lived here.

5 Stanhope Gate, Hyde Park, W1
Westminster   1911

RATCLIFF CROSS
See WILLOUGHBY, Sir Hugh

RATHBONE, Eleanor (1872–1946),
pioneer of family allowances, lived here.

Tufton Court, Tufton Street, SW1
Westminster   1986

READING, 1st Marquess of
See ISAACS, Rufus

RED HOUSE,
built in 1859–1860 by Philip WEBB, architect for William MORRIS, poet and artist who lived here 1860–1865.

Red House Lane, Bexleyheath
Bexley   1969

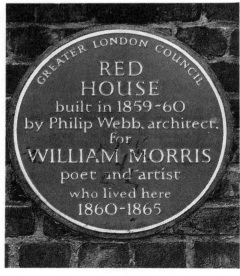

RELPH, Harry (1851–1928),
'Little Tich', music hall comedian, lived and died here.

93 Shirehall Park, Hendon, NW4
Barnet   1969

RESCHID, Mustapha Pasha (1800–1858),
Turkish statesman and reformer, lived here as an ambassador in 1839.

1 Bryanston Square, W1
Westminster   1972

REYNOLDS, Sir Joshua (1723–1792),
portrait painter, lived and died in a house on this site.

Replaces plaque put up in 1875 by RSA on building now demolished. Present plaque first erected 1947, and re-erected 1960 after completion of extensions to Fanum House.

Fanum House (site of 47), Leicester Square, WC2
Westminster   1960

RICHMOND, George (1809–1896),
painter, lived here 1843–1896.

20 York Street, W1
Westminster   1961

RICKETTS, Charles.
In these studios lived and worked the artists: Charles RICKETTS (1866–1931), Charles SHANNON (1863–1937), Glyn PHILPOT (1863–1937), Vivian FORBES (1891–1937), James PRYDE (1866–1941), F. Cayley ROBINSON (1862–1927).

Lansdowne House, 80 Lansdowne Road, W11
Kensington and Chelsea   1979

RIPON, George Frederick Samuel Robinson, Marquess of (1827–1909),
statesman and Viceroy of India, lived here.

9 Chelsea Embankment, SW3
Kensington and Chelsea   1959

RIZAL, Dr José (1861–1896),

writer and national hero of the Philippines, lived here.

Replaces private plaque erected by Philippine Society in 1955.

37 Chalcot Crescent, NW1

Camden   1983

ROBERTS, Earl Fredrick Sleigh (1832–1914),

Field-Marshal, lived here.

47 Portland Place, W1

Westminster   1922

ROBINSON, F. Cayley

See RICKETTS, Charles

ROBINSON, George Frederick

See RIPON, Marquess of

ROBINSON, W. Heath

See HEATH ROBINSON

ROE, Alliott Verdon.

Under these arches Alliott Verdon ROE assembled his AVRO No.1 triplane. In July 1909 he made the first all-British powered flight from Walthamstow Marshes.

Railway arches at Walthamstow Marsh Railway Viaduct, Walthamstow Marshes, E17

Waltham Forest   1983

ROHMER, Sax, Arthur Henry Ward (1883–1959),

creator of Dr Fu Manchu, lived here.

51 Herne Hill, SE24

Southwark   1985

Here lived Samuel ROMILLY,
law reformer. Born 1757. Died 1818.
Erected privately by the Duke of Bedford. Adopted by the GLC in 1983.
21 Russell Square, WC1
Camden   c.1903

ROMNEY, George (1734–1802),
painter, lived here.
Holly Bush Hill, NW3
Camden   1908

ROSEBERY, 5th Earl (1847–1929),
Prime Minister and first Chairman of the London County Council, was born here.
20 Charles Street, W1
Westminster   1962

ROSENBERG, Isaac (1890–1918),
poet and painter, lived in the East End and studied here.
Whitechapel Library, 77 High Street, E1
Tower Hamlets   1987

ROSS, Sir James Clark (1800–1862),
polar explorer, lived here.
2 Eliot Place, Blackheath, SE3
Lewisham   1960

ROSS, Sir Ronald (1857–1932),
Nobel Laureate, discoverer of the mosquito transmission of malaria, lived here.
18 Cavendish Square, W1
Westminster   1985

ROSSETTI, Christina Georgina (1830–1894),
poetess, lived and died here.

Bronze plaque erected by the Duke of Bedford, taken over by the GLC in 1975.

30 Torrington Square, WC1
Camden   c.1913

ROSSETTI, Dante Gabriel (1828–1882),
poet and painter, born here.

Tablet fixed, 1906. Premises rebuilt and plaque refixed 1928.

110 Hallam Street, W1
Westminster   1906

ROSSETTI, Dante Gabriel.
In this house lived in 1851 Dante Gabriel Rossetti (1828–1882), poet and painter, and from 1856–1859 William MORRIS (1834–1896), poet and artist, and Sir Edward C. (Coley) BURNE-JONES (1833–1898), painter.

17 Red Lion Square, WC1
Camden   1911

ROSSETTI, Dante Gabriel (1828–1882),
poet and painter, and Algernon Charles SWINBURNE (1837–1909), poet, lived here.

16 Cheyne Walk, SW3
Kensington and Chelsea   1949

ROSSI, Charles (Felix)
See HAYDON, Benjamin

ROWLANDSON, Thomas (1757–1827),
artist and caricaturist, lived in a house on this site.

16 John Adam Street, Adelphi, WC2
Westminster   1950

ROY, Ram Mohun (1772–1833),
Indian scholar and reformer, lived here.

49 Bedford Square, WC1
Camden   1985

ROY, Major-General William (1726–1790),
founder of the Ordnance Survey, lived here.

10 Argyll Street, W1
Westminster   1979

RUSKIN, John (1819–1900),
man of letters, lived in a house on this site.

Plaque dated 1925, on a post in front garden. Replaces plaque put up in 1909 on house now demolished.

26 Herne Hill, SE24
Lambeth   1926

RUSSELL, Lord John, 1st Earl (1792–1878),
twice Prime Minister, lived here.

37 Chesham Place, SW1
Westminster   1911

RUSSELL, J. Scott
See 'GREAT EASTERN'

RUTHERFORD, Mark
See WHITE, William Hale

SACKVILLE, Charles
See BOW STREET

SALISBURY, Robert Gascoyne Cecil, 3rd Marquess of (1830–1903),
Prime Minister, lived here.
21 Fitzroy Square, W1
Camden   1965

SALVIN, Anthony (1799–1881),
architect, lived here.
11 Hanover Terrace, Regent's Park, NW1
Westminster   1990

SAN MARTIN, José de (The Liberator) (1778–1850),
Argentine soldier and statesman, stayed here.
23 Park Road, NW1
Westminster   1953

SANTLEY, Sir Charles (1834–1922),
singer, lived and died here.
13 Blenheim Road, NW8
Westminster   1935

SARTORIUS, John F. (c.1775–c.1830),
sporting painter, lived here 1807–1812.
155 Old Church Street, SW3
Kensington and Chelsea   1963

SAVAGE, James
See ESSEX STREET

SAVARKAR, Vinayak Damodar (1883–1966),
Indian patriot and philosopher, lived here.

65 Cromwell Avenue, Highgate, N6

Haringey   1985

SCAWEN-BLUNT, Wilfrid (1840–1922),
diplomat, poet and traveller, founder of Crabbet Park Arabian stud, lived here.

15 Buckingham Gate, SW1

Westminster   1979

SCHREINER, Olive (1855–1920),
author, lived here.

16 Portsea Place, W2

Westminster   1959

SCHWITTERS, Kurt (1887–1948),
artist, lived here.

39 Westmoreland Road, Barnes, SW13

Richmond   1984

Site of SCOTLAND YARD.
First headquarters of the Metropolitan Police 1829–1890.

Ministry of Agriculture building, Whitehall Place, SW1

Westminster   1979

SCOTT, Sir George Gilbert (1811–1878),
architect, lived here.

Admiral's House, Admiral's Walk, Hampstead, NW3

Camden   1910

SCOTT, Sir Giles Gilbert (1880–1960),
architect, designed this house and lived here 1926–1960.

Chester House, Clarendon Place, W2

Westminster   1990

SCOTT, John
See ELDON, Lord

SCOTT Captain, Robert Falcon (1868–1912),
Antarctic explorer, lived here.

56 Oakley Street, SW3
Kensington and Chelsea   1935

SCOTT RUSSELL, J.
See 'GREAT EASTERN'

SEACOLE, Mary (1805–1881),
Jamaican nurse, heroine of the Crimean War, lived here.

157 George Street, Marylebone, W1
Westminster   1985

SHACKLETON, Sir Ernest Henry (1874–1922),
Antarctic explorer, lived here.

12 Westwood Hill, SE26
Lewisham   1928

SHANNON, Charles
See RICKETTS, Charles

SHARP, Cecil (1859–1924),
collector of English folk songs and dances, lived here.

4 Maresfield Gardens, NW3
Camden   1985

SHAW, George Bernard,
lived in this house from 1887–1898. 'From the coffers of his genius he enriched the world.'

Bronze plaque erected by St. Pancras Borough Council, taken over by the GLC in 1975.

29 Fitzroy Square, W1
Camden   1951

SHAW, George Bernard
See ADELPHI TERRACE

This house, designed by R. NORMAN SHAW,
architect for Frederick GOODALL, painter, was later the
home of W.S. GILBERT, writer and librettist.

Grims Dyke, Old Redding, Harrow Weald

Harrow   1976

SHELLEY, Percy Bysshe (1792–1822),
poet, lived here.

15 Poland Street, W1

Westminster   1979

SHEPHERD, Thomas Hosmer (1793–1864),
artist who portrayed London, lived here.

26 Batchelor Street, N1

Islington   1976

SHERATON, Thomas (1751–1806),
furniture designer, lived here.

163 Wardour Street, W1

Westminster   1954

SHERIDAN, Richard Brinsley,
dramatist, lived here, b.1751, d.1816.

14 Savile Row, W1

Westminster   1881

SHERIDAN, Richard Brinsley (1751–1816),
dramatist and statesman, lived here 1795–1802.
For another plaque at this address see BURGOYNE.

10 Hertford Street, W1

Westminster   1955

SHORT, Sir Frank (1857–1945),
engraver and painter, lived here.

56 Brook Green, W6

Hammersmith and Fulham   1951

SICKERT, Walter (1860–1942),
painter and etcher, lived and worked here.
6 Mornington Crescent, NW1
Camden   1977

The SILVER STUDIO,
established here in 1880. Arthur SILVER (1853–1886), Rex SILVER (1879–1965), Harry SILVER (1881–1971), designers, lived here.
84 Brook Green Road, W6
Hammersmith and Fulham   1981

SIMON, Sir John (1816–1904),
pioneer of public health, lived here.
40 Kensington Square, W8
Kensington and Chelsea   1959

SLOANE, Sir Hans.
The ground to the West of this building was given to the Parish of Chelsea in 1733 by Sir Hans Sloane, President of the Royal Society. Born 1660. Died 1753.
Kings Mead, King's Road, SW3
Kensington and Chelsea   1977

SLOANE, Sir Hans (1660–1753),
physician and benefactor of the British Museum, lived here 1695–1742.
4 Bloomsbury Place, WC1
Camden   1965

SMILES, Samuel (1812–1904),
author of 'Self Help', lived here.
11 Granville Park, SE13
Lewisham   1959

SMIRKE, Sir Robert (1781–1867),
architect, lived here.

81 Charlotte Street, W1
Camden   1979

SMITH, F.E., Earl of Birkenhead (1872–1930),
lawyer and statesman, lived here.

32 Grosvenor Gardens, SW1
Westminster   1959

SMITH, Sydney (1771–1845),
author and wit, lived here.

This plaque replaces one erected in 1905.

14 Doughty Street, WC1
Camden   1906

SMITH, William, MP (1756–1835),
pioneer of religious liberty, lived here.

16 Queen Anne's Gate, SW1
Westminster   1975

SMITH, W.H. (1825–1891),
bookseller and statesman, lived here.

This plaque was originally erected at 3 Grosvenor Place, Westminster in 1961 and removed from there in 1964.

12 Hyde Park Street, W2
Westminster   1966

SMOLLETT, Tobias
See CHELSEA CHINA

SOMERSET, Lord Fitzroy
See RAGLAN

SPURGEON, Charles Haddon (1834–1892),
preacher, lived here.

99 Nightingale Lane, SW12
Wandsworth   1971

STANFIELD, Clarkson
See PEPYS, Samuel

STANFORD, Sir Charles (1852–1924),
musician, lived here 1894–1916.
56 Hornton Street, W8
Kensington and Chelsea   1961

STANHOPE, Charles, 3rd Earl (1753–1816),
reformer and inventor, lived here.
20 Mansfield Street, W1
Westminster   1951

STANLEY, Albert Henry
See ASHFIELD, Lord

STANLEY, E.G., Earl of Derby
See PITT, W.

STANLEY, Sir Henry Morton (1841–1904),
explorer and writer, lived and died here.
2 Richmond Terrace, Whitehall, SW1
Westminster   1987

STEER, Philip Wilson (1860–1942),
painter, lived and died here.
109 Cheyne Walk, SW10
Kensington and Chelsea   1967

STEPHEN, Sir Leslie (1832–1904),
scholar and writer, lived here.
22 Hyde Park Gate, SW7
Kensington and Chelsea   1960

STEPHEN, Virginia (Virginia Woolf) (1882–1941),
novelist and critic, lived here 1907–1911.
29 Fitzroy Square, W1
Camden   1974

STEPHENSON, Robert (1803–1859),
engineer, died here.

35 Gloucester Square, W2
Westminster   1905

STEVENS, Alfred (1817–1875),
artist, lived here.

9 Eton Villas, NW3
Camden   1924

STOKER, Bram (1847–1912),
author of 'Dracula', lived here.

18 St Leonard's Terrace, SW3

Kensington and Chelsea   1977

·STOTHARD, Thomas (1755–1834),
painter and illustrator, lived here.

28 Newman Street, W1

Westminster   1911

STRACHEY, Lytton (1880–1932),
critic and biographer, lived here.

51 Gordon Square, WC1

Camden   1971

STRANG, William (1859–1921),
painter and etcher, lived here 1900–1921.

20 Hamilton Terrace, NW8

Westminster   1962

STREET, George Edmund (1824–1881),
architect, lived here.

14 Cavendish Place, W1

Westminster   1980

STRYPE STREET.
Formerly Strype's Yard, derives its name from the fact that
the house of John STRYPE, silk merchant, was situated there.
At that house was born in 1643 his son John STRYPE,
historian and biographer, who died in 1737.

10 Leyden Street, E1

Tower Hamlets   1929

STUART, Prince Charles Edward
See ESSEX STREET

STUART, John McDouall (1815–1866),
first explorer to cross Australia, lived and died here.

9 Campden Hill Square, W8

Kensington and Chelsea   1962

SWINBURNE, Algernon Charles (1837–1909),
poet, and his friend, Theodore WATTS-DUNTON
(1832–1914), poet, novelist, critic, lived and died here.

11 Putney Hill, SW15

Wandsworth   1926

SWINBURNE, A.C.
See also ROSSETTI, D.G.

SZABO, Violette, GC (1921–1945),
secret agent, lived here. She gave her life for the French
Resistance.

18 Burnley Road, Stockwell, SW9

Lambeth   1981

TAGLIONI, Marie (1809–1884),
ballet dancer, lived here in 1875–1876.

14 Connaught Square, W2

Westminster   1960

TAGORE, Rabindranath (1861–1941),
Indian poet, stayed here in 1912.

3 Villas on the Heath, Vale of Health, Hampstead,
NW3

Camden   1961

TALLEYRAND, Prince (1754–1838),
French statesman and diplomatist, lived here.

21 Hanover Square, W1

Westminster   1978

TALLIS, John (1816–1876),
publisher of 'London Street View', lived here.
233 New Cross Road, SE14
Lewisham   1978

TATE, Harry (Ronald MacDonald Hutchison) (1872–1940),
music hall comedian, lived here.
72 Longley Road, SW17
Wandsworth   1984

TAWNEY, Richard Henry (1880–1962),
historian, teacher and political writer, lived here.
21 Mecklenburgh Square, WC1
Camden   1980

TELEVISION.
The world's first regular high definition television service was inaugurated here by the BBC 2nd November 1936. *Open to the public.*
Alexandra Palace, Wood Green, N22
Haringey   1977

TEMPEST, Dame Marie (1864–1942),
actress, lived here 1899–1902.
24 Park Crescent, W1
Westminster   1972

TEMPLE, Henry John
See PALMERSTON

TERRY, Dame Ellen (1847–1928),
actress, lived here.
22 Barkston Gardens, SW5
Kensington and Cheslea   1951

THACKERAY, William Makepeace,
novelist, lived here. Born 1811, died 1863.

2 Palace Green, W8

Kensington and Chelsea   1887

THACKERAY, William Makepeace (1811–1863),
novelist, lived here.

16 Young Street, W8

Kensington and Chelsea   1905

THACKERAY, William Makepeace (1811–1863),
novelist, lived here 1854–1862.

36 Onslow Square, SW7

Kensington and Chelsea   1912

THEATRE, The
See PRIORY OF ST. JOHN THE BAPTIST

THOMAS, Dylan (1914–1953),
poet, lived here.

54 Delancey Street, NW1

Camden   1983

THOMAS, Edward (1878–1917),
essayist and poet, lived here.

61 Shelgate Road, SW11

Wandsworth   1949

THORNE, Will (1857–1946),
trade union leader and Labour MP, lived here.

1 Lawrence Road, West Ham, E13

Newham   1987

THORNYCROFT, Sir Hamo (1850–1925),
sculptor, lived here.

2a Melbury Road, W14

Kensington and Chelsea   1957

TILAK, Lokamanya (1856–1920),
Indian patriot and philosopher, lived here 1918–1919.
10 Howley Place, W2
Westminster   1988

TOWLE, Arthur
See LUCAN, Arthur

TOWNLEY, Charles (1737–1805),
antiquary and collector, lived here.
14 Queen Anne's Gate, SW1
Westminster   1985

TREE, Sir Herbert Beerbohm (1853–1917),
actor-manager, lived here.
31 Rosary Gardens, SW7
Kensington and Chelsea   1950

TROLLOPE, Anthony (1815–1882),
novelist, lived here.
39 Montagu Square, W1
Westminster   1914

TURNER, Charles (1774–1857),
engraver, lived here.
56 Warren Street, W1
Camden   1924

TURNER, J.M.W., RA (1775–1851),
painter, designed and lived in this house.
40 Sandycombe Road, Twickenham
Richmond   1977

TWAIN, Mark (Samuel Langhorne Clemens) (1835–1910),
American writer, lived here in 1896–1897.

23 Tedworth Square, SW3
Kensington and Chelsea   1960

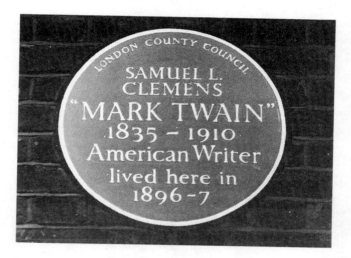

TWEED, John (1863–1933),
sculptor, lived here.

108 Cheyne Walk, SW10
Kensington and Chelsea   1985

TYBURN TREE,
site of Tyburn Tree.

Traffic Island at the junction of Edgware Road and Bayswater Road, W2
Westminster   1965

UNDERHILL, Evelyn (1875–1941),
Christian philosopher and teacher lived here 1907–1939.
Replaces plaque put up in 1975.

50 Campden Hill Square, W8
Kensington and Chelsea   1990

Mark Twain *see previous page*

UNITED STATES EMBASSY (1863–1866),
Henry Brook ADAMS (1838–1918), US historian, lived here.

98 Portland Place, W1
Westminster   1978

UNWIN, Sir Stanley (1884–1968),
publisher, was born here.

13 Handen Road, SE12
Lewisham   1984

VAN BUREN, Martin (1782–1862),
eighth US President, lived here.

7 Stratford Place, W1
Westminster   1977

VAN GOGH, Vincent (1853–1890),
painter, lived here 1873–1874.

87 Hackford Road, SW9
Lambeth   1973

Vincent Van Gogh *see previous page*

VANE, Sir Harry, the younger,
statesman, lived here. Born 1612, beheaded 1662.
House demolished but plaque remains on surviving gate pier.
Vane House, Rosslyn Hill, NW3
Camden 1897

VAUGHAN WILLIAMS, Ralph (1872–1958),
composer, lived here from 1953 until his death.
10 Hanover Terrace, Regent's Park, NW1
Westminster 1972

VENTRIS, Michael (1922–1956),
architect and decipherer of Linear B script, lived here.
19 North End, Hampstead, NW3
Camden 1990

VON HUGEL, Baron Friedrich (1852–1925),
theologian, lived here 1882–1903.
4 Holford Road, NW3
Camden 1968

WAINWRIGHT, Lincoln Stanhope (1847–1929),
Vicar of St. Peter's, London Docks, lived here 1884–1929.
Clergy House, Wapping Lane, E1
Tower Hamlets 1961

WAKLEY, Thomas (1795–1862),
reformer and founder of 'The Lancet', lived here.
35 Bedford Square, WC1
Camden 1962

WALKER, Sir Emery (1851–1933),
typographer and antiquary, lived here 1903–1933.
7 Hammersmith Terrace, W6
Hammersmith and Fulham 1959

WALLACE, Alfred Russel (1823–1913),
naturalist, lived here.

44 St. Peter's Road
Croydon   1979

WALLACE, Edgar (1875–1932),
writer, lived here.

6 Tressillian Crescent, SE4
Lewisham   1960

WALPOLE, Sir Robert (1676–1745),
Prime Minister, and his son Horace WALPOLE (1717–1797),
connoisseur and man of letters, lived here.

Replaces plaque erected by RSA in 1881 to Sir Robert Walpole alone.
5 Arlington Street, SW1
Westminster   1976

WALTER, John (1739–1812),
founder of 'The Times', lived here.

113 Clapham Common North Side, SW4
Wandsworth   1977

WARD, Arthur Henry
See ROHMER, Sax

WARLOCK, Peter, Philip Arnold Hesseltine
(1894–1930),
composer, lived here.

30 Tite Street, SW3
Kensington and Chelsea   1984

WATERHOUSE, Alfred (1830–1905),
architect, lived here.

61 New Cavendish Street, W1
Westminster   1988

WATTS-DUNTON, Theodore
See SWINBURNE, A.C.

WAUGH, Benjamin (1839–1908),
founder of the National Society for the Prevention of Cruelty to Children, lived here.

26 Croom's Hill, SE10
Greenwich   1984

WEBB, Philip
See RED HOUSE

WEBB, Sidney (1859–1947)
and Beatrice WEBB (1858–1943), social scientists and political reformers, lived here.

10 Netherhall Gardens, NW3
Camden   1981

WEIZMANN, Chaim (1874–1952),
scientist and statesman. First President of the state of Israel, lived here.

67 Addison Road, W14
Kensington and Chelsea   1980

WELLCOME, Sir Henry (1853–1936),
pharmacist, founder of the Wellcome Trust and Foundation, lived here.

6 Gloucester Gate, NW1
Camden   1989

WELLS, H.G. (1866–1946),
writer, lived and died here.

13 Hanover Terrace, NW1
Westminster   1966

WESLEY, Charles (1707–1788),
divine and hymn writer, lived and died in a house on this site, and his sons Charles (1757–1834), and Samuel (1766–1837), musicians, also lived here.

1 Wheatley Street, W1
Westminster   1953

WESLEY, John (1703–1791),
evangelist and founder of Methodism, lived here.
47 City Road, EC1
Islington   1926

WESTMACOTT, Sir Richard (1775–1856),
sculptor, lived and died here.
14 South Audley Street, W1
Westminster   1955

WHALL, Christopher Whitworth (1849–1924),
stained glass artist, lived here.
19 Ravenscourt Road, W6
Hammersmith and Fulham   1983

WHEATSTONE, Sir Charles (1802–1875),
scientist and inventor, lived here.
19 Park Crescent, W1
Westminster   1981

WHISTLER, James Abbot McNeil (1834–1903),
painter and etcher, lived here.
96 Cheyne Walk, SW10
Kensington and Chelsea   1925

WHITE, William Hale (Mark Rutherford)
(1831–1913),
novelist, lived here.
19 Park Hill, Carshalton,
Sutton   1979

WILBERFORCE, William
and the Clapham Sect worshipped in this church. Their
campaigning resulted in the abolition of slavery in the
British Dominions 1833.
Holy Trinity Church, Clapham Common, SW4
Lambeth   1984

WILBERFORCE, William (1759–1833).

On the site behind this house stood until 1904 Broomwood House – formerly Broomfield – where William Wilberforce resided during the campaign against slavery which he successfully conducted in Parliament.

111 Broomwood Road, SW11

Wandsworth   1906

WILBERFORCE, William (1759–1833),

opponent of slavery, died here.

44 Cadogan Place, SW1

Kensington and Chelsea   1961

WILDE, Oscar O'Flahertie Wills (1854–1900),

wit and dramatist, lived here.

34 Tite Street, SW3

Kensington and Chelsea   1954

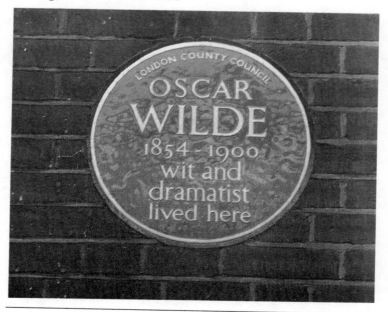

Oscar Wilde *see previous page*

WILLAN, Dr Robert (1757–1812),
dermatologist, lived here.
10 Bloomsbury Square, WC1
Camden   1949

WILLIS, 'Father' Henry (1821–1901),
organ builder, lived here.
9 Rochester Terrace, NW1
Camden   1986

WILLOUGHBY, Sir Hugh.
This plaque is in memory of Sir Hugh WILLOUGHBY
(d.1554), Stephen BOROUGH (1525–1585), William
BOROUGH (1536–1599), Sir Martin FROBISHER
(1535?–1594), and other navigators who, in the latter half of
the sixteenth century, set sail from this reach of the River
Thames near Ratcliff Cross to explore the Northern Seas.
King Edward Memorial Park, Shadwell, E1
Tower Hamlets   1922

WILSON, Edward Adrian (1872–1912),
Antarctic explorer and naturalist, lived here.
Battersea Vicarage, 42 Vicarage Crescent, SW11
Wandsworth   1935

WINANT, John Gilbert (1889–1947),
United States Ambassador 1941–1946, lived here.
7 Aldford Street, W1
Westminster   1982

WINGFIELD, Major Walter Clopton (1833–1912),
father of lawn tennis, lived here.
33 St. George's Square, SW1
Westminster   1987

WODEHOUSE, P.G. (1881–1975),
writer, lived here.
17 Dunraven Street, W1
Westminster   1988

WOLFE, General James (1727–1759),
victor of Quebec, lived here.
Macartney House, Greenwich Park, SE10
Greenwich   1909

WOLSELEY, Garnet, 1st Viscount (1833–1913),
Field-Marshal, lived in this house.
Open to the public.
Rangers House, Chesterfield Walk, Blackheath, SE10
Greenwich   1937

WOOD, Sir Henry (1869–1944),
musician, lived here.
4 Elsworthy Road, NW3
Camden   1969

WOOLF, Leonard and Virginia
lived in this house 1915–1924 and founded the Hogarth Press in 1917.
Hogarth House, Paradise Road
Richmond   1976

WOOLF, Virginia
See STEPHEN, Virginia

WYATT, Thomas Henry (1807–1880),
architect, lived and died here.
77 Great Russell Street, WC1
Camden   1980

WYATVILLE, Sir Jeffry (1766–1840),
architect, lived and died here.
39 Brook Street, Mayfair, W1
Westminster   1984

WYCHERLEY, William
See BOW STREET

WYNDHAM, Sir Charles (1837–1919),
actor-manager, lived and died here.
20 York Terrace East, NW1
Westminster   1962

YEATS, William Butler (1865–1939),
Irish poet and dramatist, lived here.
23 Fitzroy Road, NW1
Camden   1957

YOUNG, Thomas (1773–1829),
man of science, lived here.
Replaces first plaque put up in 1905.
48 Welbeck Street, W1
Westminster   1951

ZANGWILL, Israel (1864–1926),
writer and philanthropist, lived here.
288 Old Ford Road, Bethnal Green, E2
Tower Hamlets   1965

ZOFFANY, Johann (1733–1810),
painter, lived here 1790–1810.
65 Strand-on-the-Green, Chiswick, W4
Hounslow   1973

ZOLA, Emile (1840–1902),
French novelist, lived here 1898–1899.

Queen's Hotel, 122 Church Road, Upper Norwood, SE19
Croydon   1990

List of Plaques by Borough

Barnet
Blake
Hess
Johnson
Linnell
Pick
Relph

Bexley
Castlereagh
Morris
Red House
Webb

Brent
Lucan

Bromley
Grace
Kropotkin
Muirhead

Camden
Baillie, J.
Barnett
Besant, Sir W.
Brailsford
Burne-Jones
Butt
Butterfield
Caldecott
Carlyle
Cavendish
Cockerell
Constable
Cruikshank

Dale
Dance
Darwin
Dickens
Disraeli
Du Maurier, G.
Du Maurier, Sir G.
Earnshaw
Eastlake
Edwards
Eldon
Engels
Fabian Society, The
Fawcett
Ferrier
Flinders
Freud
Gaitskell
Galsworthy
Greenaway
Hammond, B.
Hammond, J.L.
Harmsworth
Harrison
Hawkins
Herford
Hill
Hodgkin
Howard
Hughes, H.P.
Hyndman
Karsavina
Keats
Keynes
Lawrence, D.H.
Lethaby

Madox Brown
Macdonald
Mansfield
Marsden
Matthay
Maxim
Mayhew
Mazzini
Mondrian
Morrell
Morris
Murry
Orwell
Patmore
Pearson, K.
Perceval
Petrie
Rackham
Rizal
Romilly
Romney
Rossetti, C.
Rossetti, D.G.
Roy
Salisbury
Scott, Sir G.
Scott, John
Sharp
Shaw
Sickert
Sloane
Smirke
Smith S.
Stephen, V.
Stevens
Strachey

Hudson
Hunt
James
Jellicoe
Jinnah
John, A.
Jordan
Kingsley
Kossuth
Lang
Langtry
Lavery
Lecky
Leighton
Lewis
Lind
Macaulay, Lord
Mallarmé
Maxwell
May
Meredith
Mill
Millais
Milne
Nehru
Orpen
Palmer
Pankhurst
Parry
Philpot
Place
Playfair
Pryde
Quaid i Azam
Ricketts
Ripon
Robinson
Rossetti, D.G.
Sartorius
Scott, R.F.
Shannon
Simon
Sloane
Smollett
Stanford
Steer
Stephen, Sir L.
Stoker
Stuart
Terry
Thackeray

Thornycroft
Tree
Twain
Tweed
Underhill
Warlock
Weizmann
Whistler
Wilberforce
Wilde

Lambeth
Barry
Baylis
Bentley
Bligh
Clapham Sect, The
County Hall, The
Cox
Ellis
Greet
Henderson
Hobbs
Inner London
  Education Authority
Leno
Montgomery
Macaulay, Z.
Ruskin
Szabo
Van Gogh
Wilberforce

Lewisham
Baird
Flecker
Glaisher
Horniman
Ross, Sir J.C.
Shackleton
Smiles
Tallis
Unwin
Wallace, E.

Merton
Innes

Newham
Thorne

Redbridge
Attlee
Mansbridge

Richmond-upon-Thames
Fielding
Garrick
Newman
Schwitters
Turner, J.M.W.
Woolf, L.
Woolf, V.

Southwark
Baird
Besant, A.
Chamberlain, J.
Drysdale
Forester
Oliver
Rohmer

Sutton
White

Tower Hamlets
Barnardo
Borough, S.
Borough, W.
Bradlaugh
Brunel, I.K.
Cavell
Cook
Frobisher
Gandhi
Gertler
'Great Eastern'
Green
Groser
Hughes, Mary
London's First Flying
  Bomb
Mallon
Rosenberg
Russell, J.S.
Strype, John
Strype Street
Wainwright
Willoughby
Zangwill

Waltham Forest
Plaatje
Roe, A.V.

Wandsworth
Benes
Burns
Douglas
Elen
Eliot, George
Hardy
Henty
Hopkins
Knee
Lauder
Lloyd George
Oates
Spurgeon
Swinburne
Tate
Thomas, E.
Walter
Watts-Dunton
Wilberforce
Wilson

Westminster
Adam, J.
Adam, R.
Adams
Adelphi Terrace
Alma-Tadema
Arkwright
Arne
Arnold, M.
Ashfield, Lord
Asquith
Astor
Avebury
Bagehot
Baird
Bairnsfather
Baldwin
Balfe
Banks
Barbon
Barrie
Basevi
Bazalgette
Beardsley
Beatty

Beauclerk, T.
Beauclerk, Lady D.
Beaufort
Beecham
Benedict
Ben-Gurion
Bentham
Berlioz
Birkenhead
Blunt
Boswell
Bow Street
Bridgeman, C.
Bridgeman, Sir O.
Bright
Brooke
Brown
Browning, E.B.
Brummell
Burgoyne
Burke
Burnett
Burney
Campbell
Campbell-Bannerman
Canaletto
Canning
Cato Street Conspiracy
Cayley
Cecil
Chamberlain, N.
Charles Edward Stuart
Chatham
Chippendale
Chopin
Churchill, Lord R.
Clarkson
Clive
Cobden
Cochrane
Coleridge
Collins
Conrad
Cons
Crosby
Cubitt
Curzon
Dadd
D'Arblay
Davies
De Gaulle

De Quincey
Derby
Disraeli
Don
Dorset
D'Oyly Carte
Dryden
Dundonald
Essex Street
Etty
Ewart
Faraday
Fielding, H.
Fielding, Sir J.
Fisher
Flaxman
Fleming
Fox
Frampton
Franklin
Free French
Friese-Greene
Frith
Fuseli
Gainsborough
Galsworthy
Galton
Garrett Anderson
Garrick
Gibbon
Gibbons
Gladstone
Godley
Gray
Green
Grey
Grossmith, G. (*Senior*)
Grossmith, G. (*Junior*)
Grote
Haldane
Hallam
Handel
Handley
Hardy
Harley
Harte
Haydon
Hazlitt
Heine
Herzen
Hill

Hogg
Hood
Hore-Belisha
Hunter, J.
Hunter, W.
Huskisson
Hutchinson
Huxley
Irving, Sir H.
Irving, W.
Isaacs
Jackson
Jerome
Johnson
Jones
Kipling
Kitchener
Klein
Knight, H.
Knight, Dame L.
Kokoschka
Lawrence, Susan
Lawrence, T.E.
Lear
Lindsey
Linnean Society
Lister
Loudon, J.C.
Loudon, Jane
Lubbock
Lugard
Lutyens
Lyell
Macklin
Malone
Manby
Manning
Manson
Marconi
Marryat
Marx
Maugham
Maurice
Metternich
Meynell
Millbank Prison
Milner
Montefiore

Moore, G.
Moore, T.
Morse
Mozart
Napoleon III
Nelson
Newton
Nightingale
Nollekens
Novello
Onslow
Orford
Oxford
Palgrave
Palmerston, Viscount
Patel
Peabody
Pearson, J.L.
Peel
Pepys
Pinero
Pitt (Chatham)
Pitt (*the younger*)
Pitt-Rivers
Pombal, Marquess of
Portuguese Embassy
Radcliffe
Raglan
Rathbone
Reading
Reschid
Reynolds
Richmond
Roberts
Rosebery
Ross, Sir R.
Rossetti, D.G.
Rossi
Rowlandson
Roy
Russell, Lord J.
Sackville
Salvin
San Martin
Santley
Savage
Scawen-Blunt
Schreiner

Scotland Yard
Scott, Sir Giles
Seacole
Shaw
Shelley
Sheraton
Sheridan
Smith, F.E.
Smith, William
Smith, W.H.
Somerset, Lord
Stanfield
Stanhope
Stanley, E.G.
Stanley, Sir H.M.
Stephenson
Stothard
Strang
Street
Taglioni
Talleyrand
Tempest
Temple
Tilak
Townley
Trollope
Tyburn Tree
United States Embassy
Van Buren
Vaughan Williams
Walpole, H.
Walpole, Sir R.
Wells
Waterhouse
Wesley, C.
Wesley, C. (*the younger*)
Wesley, S.
Westmacott
Wheatstone
Winant
Wingfield
Wodehouse
Wyatville
Wycherley
Wyndham
Young

List of People by Vocation

Applied Arts
Brummell
Chippendale
Cobden-Sanderson
De Morgan, E.
De Morgan, W.
Johnston
Morris
Sheraton
Short
Silver
Stevens
Turner, C.
Walker
Whall

Archaeology and Ethnography
Avebury
Horniman
Kingsley, M.
Petrie
Pitt-Rivers
Townley
Ventris

Architecture and Building
Adam, J.
Adam, R.
Barbon
Barry
Basevi
Bentley
Butterfield
Campbell

Cockerell
Cubitt
Dance
Freake
Godwin
Hansom
Lethaby
Lutyens
Pearson
Salvin
Savage
Scott, Sir George
Scott, Sir Giles
Shaw
Smirke
Street
Ventris
Waterhouse
Webb, P.
Wyatt
Wyatville

Armed Forces
Allenby
Baden-Powell
Beatty
Burgoyne
Cochrane
Fisher
Fitzroy
Jellicoe
Kitchener
Lawrence, T.E.
Nelson
Raglan
Roberts

Roy, W.
Szabo
Wolfe
Wolseley

Aviation
Johnson
Roe

British Overseas
Brooke
Cavell
Clive
Curzon
Godley
Lugard
Milner
Ripon

Cartoonists and Illustrators
Bairnsfather
Beardsley
Beerbohm
Caldecott
Crane
Cruikshank
Greenaway
Heath Robinson
Lear
McGill
May
Rackham
Rowlandson
Stothard

Civil Engineers
Bazalgette
Brunel, I.
Brunel, M.
Manby
Stephenson

Education
Davies, E.
Hogg
McMillan
Mansbridge

Fine Arts
Alma-Tadema
Beauclerk, D.
Blake
Brangwyn
Burne-Jones
Canaletto
Constable
Cox
Dadd
Eastlake
Etty
Fildes
Forbes
Frith
Fuseli
Gainsborough
Gertler
Goodall
Greaves
Haydon
John
Knight, H.
Knight, L.
Kokoschka
Lavery
Leighton
Lewis
Linnell
Madox Brown
Millais
Mondrian
Morse
Orpen
Palmer
Philpot
Pissarro
Pryde

Reynolds
Richmond
Ricketts
Robinson
Romney
Rosenberg
Rossetti, D.G.
Sartorius
Schwitters
Shannon
Shepherd
Sickert
Stanfield
Steer
Strang
Turner, J.M.W.
Van Gogh
Whistler
Zoffany

Gardening
Bridgeman, C.
Innes
Linnean Society
Loudon

Historians
Belloc
Besant, W.
Brailsford
Carlyle
Froude
Gibbon
Green
Grote
Hallam
Hammond, B.
Hammond, J.L.
Lecky
Macaulay, T.B.
Strype
Tawney

Historical Sites
Adelphi Terrace
Alexandra Palace
Bow Street
Cato Street
Chelsea China
Congregational
  Memorial Hall

County Hall
Essex Street
Fabian Society
Flying Bomb
Free French
Greater London
  Council
Horniman Museum
Inner London
  Education Authority
Labour Party
Linnean Society
London County
  Council
Millbank Prison
Portuguese Embassy
Priory of St. John the
  Baptist
Red House
A.V. Roe
Scotland Yard
Silver Studio
Strype Street
Theatre, The
Toynbee Hall
Tyburn
United States Embassy

**Industry and
Invention**
Arkwright
Baird
Blumlein
Caslon
Creed
Earnshaw
Friese-Greene
Hansom
Harrison
Marconi
Maxim
Morse
Muirhead
Peel
Roe
Stanhope

**Journalism and
Publishing**
Arnold, E.
Davies, T.

Edwards
Harmsworth
Mayhew
Tallis
Unwin
Walter

Law
Bridgeman, O.
Eldon
Fielding, J.
Haldane
Isaacs
Romilly
Smith, F.E.

Literature
Beauclerk, T.
Belloc
Boswell
Chesterton
De Quincey
Dickinson
Dobson
Du Maurier, George
Gosse
Hawthorne
Hazlitt
Irving, W.
Jefferies
Jerome
Johnson
Lamb
Lang
Malone
Morrell
Murry
Palgrave
Pepys
Ruskin
Schreiner
Smiles
Smith, S.
Stephen
Strachey
Walpole, H.

Medicine
Barnardo
Bright
Cavell

Dale
Drysdale
Ellis
Fleming
Freud
Garrett Anderson
Gray
Hodgkin
Hunter, J.
Hunter, W.
Hutchinson
Huxley
Jackson
Jones
Klein
Lister
Manson
Marsden
Nightingale
Radcliffe
Ross
Seacole
Sloane
Wakley
Wellcome
Willan

Music and Dance
Arne
Astafieva
Balfe
Beecham
Benedict
Berlioz
Bridge
Butt
Chopin
Clementi
Coleridge-Taylor
Elgar
Ferrier
Gounod
Handel
Hess
Karsavina
Lind
Matthay
Mozart
Parry
Santley
Sharp

Stanford
Taglioni
Vaughan Williams
Warlock
Willis
Wood

Music Hall and Radio
Chevalier
Collins, S.
Elen
Handley
Lauder
Leno
Leybourne
Lloyd
Lucan
Relph
Tate

Novelists
Ballantyne
Beerbohm
Bennett
Burnett
Burney
Collins, W.
Conan-Doyle
Conrad
Defoe
Dickens
Douglas
Eliot, George
Fielding, H.
Ford
Forester
Forster
Galsworthy
Gaskell
Gissing
Grahame
Haggard
Hardy
Harte
Hawkins
Henty
Hudson
James
Kingsley, C.
Kipling
Lawrence, D.H.

Mansfield
Marryat
Maugham
Meredith
Milne
Moore, G.
Orwell
'Ouida'
Rohmer
Stoker
Thackeray
Trollope
Twain
Wells
White
Wodehouse
Woolf, V.
Zola

Overseas Visitors
Adams
Benes
Berlioz
Canaletto
Chopin
Clementi
De Gaulle
Engels
Franklin
Gandhi
Gounod
Harte
Hawthorne
Heine
Herzen
Irving, W.
James
Jinnah
Kossuth
Mallarmé
Marconi
Marx
Mazzini
Metternich
Mondrian
Morse
Mozart
Napoleon III
Nehru
Patel
Patmore

Plaatje
Pombal
Reschid
Rizal
Roy, R.M.
San Martin
Savarkar
Seacole
Talleyrand
Tilak
Twain
Van Buren
Van Gogh
Weizmann
Winant
Zola

Philanthropy and Reform
Barnardo
Barnett, H.
Barnett, S.
Besant, A.
Booth
Bradlaugh
Chisholm
Edwards
Ewart
Fawcett
Horniman
Howard
Hughes
Lawrence, S.
Macaulay, Z.
Mallon
Montefiore
Oliver
Peabody
Rathbone
Simon
Smith, W.
Waugh
Wilberforce
Zangwill

Poets
Arnold, M.
Barrett
Blake
Browning
Coleridge

Dryden
Eliot, T.S.
Hardy
Heine
Hood
Hopkins
Housman
Hunt
Keats
Kipling
Mallarmé
Moore, T.
Patmore
Rosenberg
Rossetti, C.
Rossetti, D.G.
Sackville
Shelley
Swinburne
Thomas, D.
Thomas, E.
Watts-Dunton
Yeats

Political Economy
Bagehot
Engels
Galton
Herzen
Keynes
Kropotkin
Laski
Mill
Webb, B.
Webb, S.

Politics and Administration
Ashfield
Astor
Burke
Burns
Canning
Castlereagh
Cecil
Chamberlain, J.
Chesterfield
Churchill, R.
Cobden
Cripps
Crosby

Dilke
Fox
Gaitskell
Grey
Harley
Henderson
Hill
Hore-Belisha
Huskisson
Hyndman
Knee
Morrison
Onslow
Pankhurst
Place
Pick
Smith, W.H.
Stuart
Vane

Prime Ministers
Asquith
Attlee
Baldwin
Bonar Law
Campbell-Bannerman
Chamberlain, N.
Churchill
Derby
Disraeli
Gladstone
Lloyd George
MacDonald
Palmerston
Peel
Perceval
Pitt, W. (Chatham)
Pitt, W. (*the younger*)
Rosebery
Russell
Salisbury
Walpole

Religion
Barnett, S.
Carlile
Clapham Sect
Groser
Herford
Hughes
Irving, E.
Lindsey

Manning
Maurice
Newman
Priestley
Spurgeon
Underhill
Von Hugel
Wainwright
Wesley, C.
Wesley, J.

Science
Banks
Bentham
Brown
Cavendish
Cayley
Darwin
Don
Dyson
Eddington
Ellis
Faraday
Fitzroy
Fleming
Galton
Lyell
Glaisher
Gosse, P.
Huxley
Maxwell
Newton
Pearson, K.
Priestley
Wallace
Wheatstone
Young

Sculptors
Flaxman
Frampton
Gaudier-Brzeska
Gibbons
Nollekens
Rossi
Thornycroft
Tweed
Westmacott

Sport
Grace
Hobbs

Theatre
Alexander
Baillie
Barrie
Baylis
Clarkson
Cons
D'Oyly Carte
Du Maurier, Gerald
Flecker
Garrick
Gilbert
Greet
Grimaldi
Grossmith
Irving, H.
Jordan
Langtry
Novello
Phelps
Pinero
Playfair
Shaw
Sheridan
Tempest
Terry
Tree
Wilde
Wyndham

Travellers and Explorers
Beaufort
Bligh
Borough, S.
Borough, W.
Borrow
Cook
Flinders
Frobisher
Galton
Oates
Ross, J.C.
Scott, R.F.
Shackleton
Stuart
Willoughby
Wilson

Alphabetical Street Index

ALPHABETICAL STREET INDEX

Highbury Place 17
High Holborn 31
High Street,
  Whitechapel 89
Hobury Street 75
Holford Road 109
Holland Park Road
  66, 74
Holland Street 25
Holly Bush Hill 89
Holybourne Avenue
  54
Hornton Street 98
Howitt Road 71
Howley Place 104
Hyde Park Gate 3, 20,
  98
Hyde Park Street 97

Islington Green 22

Jermyn Street 79
John Adam Street 91

Keats Grove 61
Kennington Oval 76
Kensington Church
  Street 20
Kensington Court
  Gardens 33
Kensington Park
  Gardens 25
Kensington Square 75,
  81, 96
King Edward
  Memorial Park 115
King Street, Covent
  Garden 2
King Street, St.
  James's 78
King's Road 3, 45, 96

Lambeth Road 11, 46
Lancaster Gate 51
Langford Place 63
Langham Street 72
Lansdowne Road 87
Lavender Gardens 52
Lawford Road 80
Lawrence Road 103

Lawrence Street 18
Leicester Square 87
Leyden Street 100
Lincoln's Inn Fields
  73, 83
Lisson Grove 51
London Hospital 17
London Road 54
Longley Road 65, 102
Lyall Street 25

Maida Vale 40
Mallord Street 59, 76
Manchester Square 8,
  57, 76
Manchester Street 7
Mansfield Street 82, 98
Maresfield Gardens
  38, 94
Marlborough Place 56
Marloes Road 64
Mecklenburgh Square
  102
Melbury Road 35, 53,
  103
Mile End Road 24
Millbank 76
Monkhams Avenue 3
Montagu Square 104
Morden Road 44
Mornington Crescent
  96
Mortimer Road 44
Mortimer Street 79
Moss Lane 51
Mottingham Lane 44
Mount Park Road 5
Mount Vernon 26

Netherhall Gardens
  32, 111
Newark Street 46
New Bond Street 78
New Cavendish Street
  110
New Cross Road 102
Newman Street 100
Nightingale Lane 97
North End 69, 109

North Road, Highgate
  54
North Side, Clapham
  Common 14

Oakley Gardens 42
Oakley Street 94
Old Brompton Road
  68
Old Church Street 27,
  61, 92
Old Ford Road 117
Old Redding 95
Old Town, Clapham 8
Onslow Gardens 11,
  40, 66
Onslow Square 35, 103
Orme Square 52
Orsett Terrace 52
Osnaburgh Street 34
Outer Circle, Regent's
  Park 21
Outram Road 25

Palace Court 75
Palace Gardens
  Terrace 7, 68, 74
Palace Gate 75
Palace Green 103
Pall Mall 40
Pandora Road 50
Paradise Road 116
Park Crescent 69, 102,
  112
Park Hill 112
Park Lane 76
Park Road 92
Parkhill Road 76
Pavement, The 71
Pelham Crescent 84
Percy Street 82
Phillimore Place 45
Piccadilly 81
Poland Street 95
Pond Road 51
Pond Street 53
Pont Street 1, 65
Porchester Terrace 69
Portland Place 14, 88,
  106

131

Portsea Place 93
Powis Road 41
Putney Hill 101

Queen Anne Street 8
Queen Anne's Gate
35, 47, 49, 81, 97, 104
Queen Caroline Street
12
Queen's Grove 37

Ram Place 85
Ravenscourt Road 112
Ravenscourt Square 80
Red House Lane 86
Red Lion Square 50, 90
Redcliffe Street 30
Regent's Park Road 33
Richmond Terrace 98
Ridings, The 11
Robert Street 1
Rochester Ter ace 115
Rodenhurst Road 52
Rosary Gardens 104
Rosslyn Hill 109
Routh Road 69
Russell Road 58
Russell Square 89
Russell Street 60
Rutland Gate 41, 71

St. Ann's Villas 19
St. George's Square
115
St. James's Place 19, 56
St. James's Square 3,
84
St. Leonard's Terrace
100
St. Luke's Road 55
St. Martin's Lane 19
St. Peter's Road 110
Sandycombe Road 104
Savile Row 6, 13, 49,
95
Seymour Place 23
Seymour Street 5, 66
Sheffield Terrace 16
Shelgate Road 103
Shirehall Park 87

Sloane Street 28
Soho Square 5, 80
South Audley Street
112
South Bolton Gardens
80
South Eaton Place 17
South Street 3, 79
Southampton Row 68
Southwood Lane 62
Spaniards Road 6
Spanish Place 49, 73
Stafford Place 54
Stamford Brook Road
84
Stanhope Gate 86
Sterling Street 5
Stockwell Park Road 6
Stoke Newington
Church Street 27
Strand-on-the-Green
117
Stratford Place 107
Strype's Yard, Strype
Street (see Leyden
Street)
Suffolk Street 20, 26
Sugden Road 63
Sumner Place 50
Sutton Lane 37

Tavistock Street 27
Taviton Street 55
Tedworth Square 105
Tennison Road 22
Theobald's Road 30
Thurleigh Avenue 32
Tite Street 110, 113
Torrington Square 90
Tressillian Crescent
110
Trinity Road 50
Tufton Street 86
Turner Street 12

Underhill Road 37
Upper Belgrave Street
4
Upper Berkeley Street
41

Upper Cheyne Row 55
Upper Grosvenor
Street 82
Upper Harley Street 74
Upper Mall 21
Upper Richmond
Road 79

Vale of Health 49, 65,
101
Vallance Road 55
Vanbrugh Hill 31
Vicarage Crescent 115
Villiers Street 62

Walthamstow
Marshes 88
Wapping Lane 109
Wardour Street 20, 95
Warren Street 104
Warrington Crescent 8
Warwick Gardens 19
Water Lane 16
Watery Lane 56
Welbeck Street 73, 117
Well Road 82
Well Walk 23, 56
Westbourne Terrace
65, 72
Westferry Road 46
Westmoreland Road
93
Westwood Hill 94
Wetherby Gardens 2
Wheatley Street 111
Whitehall Place 93
Wildwood Road 52, 83
Wilton Place 8
Wilton Street 45
Wimbledon Park
Road 32
Wimpole Street 13, 49
Windmill Hill 4
Windsor Road 73

York Gate 80
York Street 87
York Terrace East 60,
117
Young Street 103